McDonnell Douglas Douglas DC-10

By Terry Waddington

Great AIRLINERS SERIES

Volume Six

The publisher acknowledges that certain terms, logos, names and model designations are property of the trademark holder. They are used here for correct identification purposes only.

All information contained in this volume is accurate at the time of publication.

Series Editor: Jon Proctor

Book and cover design by Randy Wilhelm, Left Field Productions, Sandpoint, Idaho
Copy Editor: Billie Jean Plaster

Unless otherwise indicated, photos are courtesy of the Boeing Historical Archives.

Note: All mileage references in the text and tables are in nautical miles.

The Great Airliners series:

TABLE OF CONTENTS

APPENDICES

Geoffrey Thomas

ACKNOWLEDGMENTS

In researching the information presented in this book, I have once again been fortunate to draw upon former McDonnell Douglas employees who were intimately involved with the subject aircraft. In particular, I was greatly assisted by several design engineers who "started with a clean sheet of paper," and created the aircraft's basic design through much iteration. John E. Morris, who headed the advanced design group and Richard Cathers, who drafted the basic outlines, both became the joint nominal holders of the DC-10 patent. Richard, in particular, had kept copies of all his drawings and notes pertaining to the design and made them available. John recalled the early airline meetings that helped determine the requirements and was the person who saw the potential in turning the original twin concept into the tri-jet. Tony Paradiso, who headed the military advanced design group and was responsible for the KC-10 design, provided material on the unclassified studies for proposed military developments of the DC-10.

Others who helped include Bob Goforth, Gerry Kingsley, Mike Machat, Paul Minnert, Brian Parkinson and Roger Schaufele. Once again, I am particularly indebted to Pat McGinnis, archivist at the Boeing-Long Beach facility, for her invaluable help. My thanks are also offered to the Boeing archivists at Seattle for information on the 1968 Boeing 747-300 tri-jet proposal.

Two friends deserve special mention. Robert (Bob) D. Archer offered significant input on the DC-10 from his MDC days and provided substantial L-1011 TriStar information gained during his sojourn at Lockheed. Again, it has been a continued pleasure to work with Jon Proctor, Great Airliners Series editor, who also came to my rescue many times with data or photos that I couldn't track down.

I hereby gratefully acknowledge the efforts of the many photographers who contributed to the cause; most are recognized in the captions where known. Some of the author's collection also came from Jeff Burch, Bruce Drum, Malcolm Gault, Martin Hornlimann, Pierre Petit and A. J. Smith. Others were acquired at the annual and regional Airliners International conventions.

Most of the air-to-air and factory scene photographs were obtained prior to the merger of MDC with Boeing, but I appreciate very much being given permission by the Boeing Historical Archives to publish them. Though legally the aircraft is now identified as the Boeing DC-10, in the interests of historical accuracy, I have used the McDonnell Douglas nomenclature except with regard to the recent Boeing MD-10F version.

This book is dedicated to the many enthusiasts worldwide who indulge in the fascinating hobby of photographing airliners in the splendid variety of color schemes. Without them, this book would not have been possible.

Terry Waddington
Roseburg, Oregon

INTRODUCTION

The evolution of a modern jet transport takes many years and the design goes through numerous twists and turns before the first production aircraft is built. The McDonnell Douglas DC-10 was initially proposed to meet a requirement for a medium-range, twin-engine transport capable of carrying up to 250 passengers. However, thanks to far-sighted thinking of some McDonnell Douglas staff, it developed into something totally different, an intercontinental range tri-jet capable of carrying 380 passengers. Fortuitously, concurrent engine development by General Electric Corporation (GE), Pratt & Whitney and Rolls-Royce kept pace with the changing requirements. Engine thrust is the primary factor that dictates the design of an airframe for a particular set of missions. In the case of the DC-10, 40,000-pound-thrust engines with potential for further development transformed it from a limited market potential – mainly comprising U.S. domestic airlines – into an aircraft that could be marketed worldwide.

Unfortunately, several factors affected the DC-10 sales totals. Throughout the development and production cycle, it encountered fierce competition from Lockheed Aircraft Company and its similarly sized L-1011 TriStar, plus Boeing's larger 747 and Airbus Industrie's A300 family. In addition, two unfortunate accidents had a major impact on the aircraft's reputation. The design was absolved by Federal Aviation Administration (FAA) and the National Transport Safety Board (NTSB) in the second case, but a downturn in the world economy affected all four manufacturers of widebody aircraft, leading to a rapid decline in sales.

Although it was replaced on the production line by the MD-11, increases in engine thrust and reliability have led to the DC-10's replacement by large, twin-engine aircraft. Many DC-10s have followed the example of the manufacturer's predecessor, the DC-8, by becoming a major factor in the air transportation of cargo worldwide, and will be seen flying the world's air lanes for many years to come.

It was the dream of James S. McDonnell to have his name on at least one commercial jet transport. In spite of some of the negative comments by the tabloid press and some officials who should have known better, he could be justly proud of the DC-10.

Chapter I
PAPER GIANTS

The Douglas D-918 was offered to Pan Am in competition with the Boeing 747. (via Richard Cathers)

In 1965, Douglas Aircraft Company (DAC) at Long Beach, California was bustling with activity. The first DC-9 rolled out in February, flight testing was proceeding rapidly and ramping up the production rate was in high gear for year-end deliveries to the type's initial purchaser, Delta Air Lines. As early concerns were quickly overcome, new orders came in at a steady pace, reaching a total of 225 by December. The company had launched the DC-9 program on April 8, 1963, with no orders in hand. The DC-8-50 production line was well established, with the last of the Series 40s also moving down the line. Although orders for the DC-8 were declining, they picked up rapidly with the launch of the Series 62 with an order from SAS, on April 4. This was quickly followed by initial orders for the Series 61 from United and Eastern; KLM ordered the first Series 63s before the end of the year. Thus, the main design office at Long Beach was busy with two programs as more airlines placed customized orders for new variants. This was to soon create major problems.

In addition to all its commercial endeavors, Douglas was producing the A-4 Skyhawk light attack bomber used by the United States Navy and Marine Corps. Skyhawk production was brisk as the Vietnam conflict expanded. The major sub-assemblies were being produced at the Long Beach plant, then shipped to Palmdale for final assembly and flight testing.

It was a banner year financially; the company returned to profitability after several years "in the red" due to the cancelled Skybolt missile program, expenditures required to fix the aerodynamic problems on the early DC-8s plus the DC-9 program start-up costs.

Advanced Design teams were already looking at further growth versions of the DC-8 and the DC-9 plus several military projects. Foremost of the tasks was a requirement, first issued in 1961, for a heavy-lift aircraft much larger than anything previously considered. This project, the Douglas D-902, was a six-engine aircraft, with a Maximum Takeoff Weight (MTOW) of 606,000 pounds, capable of carrying outsize cargo weighing 195,000 pounds over a 3,750-mile range. The need for six engines arose because the maximum engine thrust at the time was about 30,000 pounds.

The new freighter was required to replace the aging Douglas C-124 Globemaster that was nearing the end of its structural life. A full-size fuselage mock-up was built, including an unusual feature. The entire nose, including the cockpit, rotated 180 degrees to simplify cargo loading. Douglas engineers had first looked at this concept in 1958 when the then Santa Monica-based design team was reviewing proposed freighter versions of the DC-8. However, only a swing-tail version was also considered. Originally included in several large military glider designs during World War II, this characteristic was already in use on the British-built Armstrong Whitworth Argosy. Later, side-swing noses were installed on the series of re-worked Boeing 377 Stratocruisers known as Guppies and Super Guppies, modified and operated by Aero Spacelines, Inc., of Santa Barbara, California and used to carry oversize cargo.

The D-902 was a company funded project undertaken before a formal request for proposal (RFP) had been received from military authorities. A revised design was subsequently designated D-906 to properly address the RFP.

CX-HLS Competition

The U.S. Department of Defense issued a much-revised heavy-lifter proposal known as the CX-HLS (Heavy Logistics System), in December 1964. It specified four 40,000-pound-thrust, high bypass-ratio engines that were then being developed by both General Electric (GE) and Pratt & Whitney (P&W). The creation of these two engines was to be the single most important factor in the development of future large-capacity air transports.

The specification called for sufficient fuselage width to carry two rows of military vehicles side by side, with a floor strong enough to carry a main battle tank. An upper deck behind the cockpit was required to carry lighter cargo or provide troop seating. Three aircraft manufacturers, Boeing, Douglas and Lockheed, were invited to submit proposals.

The Douglas entry, designated the D-916, had an MTOW of 750,000 pounds. It was intended to haul a 125,000-pound payload over 6,800 miles. The design permitted operation onto runways of limited length and bearing strength at reduced weights, thanks to its multi-unit landing gear that distributed the tire footprints. It could also lift 250,000-pound payloads over a shorter distance. A high-mounted wing with four

The CX-HLS military proposal was the genesis of Douglas widebody transports.

pylon-suspended engines and landing gear located in pods on either side of the fuselage allowed a low, unobstructed main deck thus facilitating loading and unloading of vehicles via a built-in ramp. It also reduced runway-length requirements. The nose-loading feature differed from the earlier D-902/906 in that the high cockpit remained fixed with just the lower nose being side-hinged for main-deck access.

Civilian Projects

Lockheed won the CX-HLS competition in October 1965 with its entry that became the C-5A Galaxy. Naturally, this led both Boeing and Douglas to re-evaluate future aircraft programs. Boeing, working with Pan Am President Juan Trippe, decided to utilize the military design and research effort to build a commercial airliner of slightly smaller proportions. Lockheed also began looking at using the basic C-5A design to develop its own large airliner. Designated L-500, it featured triple decks and capacity for 902 passengers or 140 tons of cargo.

The Douglas design team evaluated its CX-HLS submission for mixed cargo/passenger operations and proposed a new double-deck fuselage to accommodate 900 passengers. The latter was identified as the D-918, and much of the work carried over onto future transport studies including the Pan Am requirement initiated by Juan Trippe.

Although Douglas devoted a substantial effort with its D-918 study, doubts existed as to when such a large aircraft should be launched. Having just made financial commitments to stretching the DC-8 and recently returning to profitability, the company was not anxious to quickly invest in yet another new program.

SST Interlude

The mid-1960s also saw a great effort undertaken with the design of supersonic transports (SST) in the United States. Triggered by the head-start development of the Anglo-French Concorde, both Douglas and Lockheed had been exploring Mach 2 SST designs since 1958. General Dynamics and Boeing joined in shortly thereafter with Mach 3 studies.

More detailed design work on American-built supersonic airliners was initiated in August 1963 when the Federal Aviation Administration (FAA) issued an RFP for a U.S.-built supersonic transport much larger and faster than the proposed Concorde. After 57 trial designs had been investigated, Douglas elected to drop out of the "Supersonic race" in September 1963 and concentrate its limited resources on the DC-9 program.

In 1964, Boeing, Lockheed and General Dynamics submitted separate Mach 3 airliner proposals to the FAA, which was sponsoring the program on behalf of the U.S. Government. Boeing was eventually awarded a

contract to proceed with its design against a growing tide of objections from environmentalists and other groups concerned about the fact that the U.S. Government was investing 75 percent of its development funds – to a maximum of $750 million – on the program.

At the time, it was widely forecast that the total worldwide seat-mile demand would exceed 235 billion per year by 1990. SSTs were expected to generate 120 billion seat-miles. The International Civil Aviation Organization (ICAO) projected that the 1965 airfreight capacity of less than 10 billion cargo ton-miles would grow to between 160 and 260 billion ton-miles by 1990. As a leading proponent of freighter aircraft, Douglas managers felt that any future large aircraft should be designed with this application in mind.

The SST program eventually succumbed to burgeoning costs and major technical difficulties such as weight and the inability to solve the sonic boom effects along its flight path that restricted the number of practical potential routes.

Two for the Price of One

When a manufacturer initiates a new design proposal, substantial time is spent talking to potential customers about their requirements before any real design effort is undertaken. So it was not until February 23,1966, that Douglas announced that it was circulating two basic proposals for its next-generation airliner. It would be called the DC-10 if either of the proposals entered production. The projects were identified as the D-950 and D-952. Though different in size, both were designed to a common basic configuration that abandoned the earlier military high wing for a low-wing position, still with four pylon-mounted engines. Neither of the designs was as large as the CX-HLS proposal. The cross-section in both cases was a double-bubble shape, but of different sizes, similar to that used on the Douglas DC-8 but on a much larger scale. Power would be provided by either the GE CF-6 or P&W JTF-14E engine, both still under development and in the 40,000-pound-thrust class. These engines were commercial outgrowths of the military engines that competed for the CX-HLS contract.

Initially, three different models of the smaller D-950 were considered:

	SEATS*	CARGO VOLUME
D-950-10	376	18,670 cubic feet
D-950-30	457	22,060 cubic feet
D-950-50	524	22,060 cubic feet
*all-economy configuration		

All versions were predicated on a maximum payload of 150,000 pounds over a 6,000-mile range. The baseline aircraft – the Series 30 – was

Basic Cross-Section Alternatives

In order to stow two 8-foot by 8-foot containers side by side, several alternate cross-sections were considered for the D-950. The DC-8 is shown on the top left for scale.

assigned a length of 194 feet, 4 inches for study purposes. The Series 10 was approximately 14 feet shorter, and the Series 50 was 12 feet longer. The wing span was 167 feet, 6 inches. The D-950's cross-section (186 inches wide) offered seven-across, twin-aisle seating (2-3-2) on the main deck. The upper deck's 136-inch width was equal to the DC-8 fuselage and offered six-across seating (3-3) with a single aisle. Overall seating and aisle widths were based on the DC-8. The seat pitch would be 34 inches with 86-inch headroom on both decks. The cargo compartments offered a 57-inch clearance.

As an all-cargo aircraft, the lower deck could accommodate two side-by-side, 88-inch by 125-inch pallets on the main deck, plus single pallets on the upper deck. Loading of the main deck was through a smaller side-swinging nose section below the cockpit. The upper deck was accessed through a side freight door with upper hinges.

The D-952 featured a much more voluminous cross-section on both levels. The main deck (206 inches wide) featured two 19-inch aisles and an eight-abreast seating (2-4-2) arrangement, while the upper deck (186 inches wide) was also in a twin-aisle layout with seven-across seating (2-3-2). The cabin ceilings on both decks were raised to 100 inches, allowing accommodation of full 8-foot by 8-foot containers in the cargo version. Two models were studied, the 182-foot-long D-952-10, and the D-952-30, which was 212 feet in length. The first example could carry a maximum of 458 passengers, versus 563 in the Dash 30. All aisle widths were increased to 20 inches. The wing of the D-952 was increased to 206 feet, 9 inches for both versions. The wing structure was similar to the D-950, but with extended tips and increased flap spans.

The Series 30 was designed to carry a 240,000-pound payload over 3,500 miles or 300,000 pounds over 2,150 miles, while the Series 10 could haul 150,000 pounds over 4,000 miles.

A Change of Plans

Just prior to Boeing's 747 program launch with an order for 25 aircraft from Pan American on April 13, 1966, Douglas declared that it had ceased development of the D-950, but would continue the low-key development of its D-952 study with rollout tentatively scheduled for 1972 and service

entry in 1975. Market researchers had concluded that an aircraft of its size was not yet viable because aircraft like the Boeing 707 and Douglas DC-8 could handle most of the long-haul traffic for some time. In addition, it was felt that:

• Very large aircraft were considered premature prior to 1975.
• Cargo was crucial to development of large aircraft as doubts existed concerning long-term passenger growth in intercontinental sub-sonic transports due to the forthcoming SSTs.
• General airline reaction currently favored a maximum passenger capacity of 280.
• A 280-350 seat aircraft powered by four 40,000-pound-thrust engines could not economically compete with the stretched Douglas DC-8s.
• Frequency and smaller capacity would meet freight requirements prior to 1975.

Juan Trippe's order for 1970 deliveries of the 747 triggered a purchasing frenzy from many airlines whose managers were afraid of being left behind. However, as history subsequently revealed, Douglas researchers were correct and the early 747 operators struggled to fill the big jets in the early 1970s, with many being mothballed or sold. Boeing was forced to lay off 80,000 employees in 1970-71 as the airline industry tried to absorb the sudden over capacity during a worldwide economic downturn.

The D-956

The Douglas decision to continue studies of large transports centered on the belief that the future still lay in airfreight growth. Emphasis was equally divided between cargo and passenger applications, marking the first time that a commercial freighter was not just a natural progression from an airliner or military specification.

Thus, the D-956 was born, leading to an even wider fuselage cross-section to allow several 8-foot by 8-foot by 10-foot containers to be carried in two rows on the main deck with ample clearance. A single row of similar containers could be carried on the upper deck. Both upper and lower lobes were increased in diameter by approximately 1 foot. This created wider aisles and the installation of wider seats in the passenger version; upper deck seating was now in a 2-3-2 layout while the main deck layout changed to a 2-4-2 arrangement. The freighter version retained the same swing-nose-loading system for the lower deck and side loading of the upper deck. The upward-hinging upper deck door was wide enough to allow 8-foot by 8-foot by 25-foot containers to be loaded at an angle.

With a common wingspan of 191 feet, three different fuselage lengths were considered. Two engine alternatives were also proposed, the GE CTF-39 and the P&W JT9D-1, both then developing 41,000 pounds of thrust. The basic models were identified as the D-956-13 or -13F (GE CTF-39) and D-956-23 or -23F (P&W JT9D-1), both with 180-foot-long fuselages. As a passenger aircraft, either could carry up to 400 passengers over a 6,500-mile range.

Stretched versions carrying more passengers over shorter ranges were also explored. Two studies – the D-956-14 (with CTF-39 engines) and the D-956-24 (with the JT9D-1) with 20-foot fuselage extensions – were designed to carry 500 passengers over 5,100 miles, but did not come to fruition. However, 602-seat, double-deck design – the D-956-15 (with GE CTF-39 power plants) or the D-956-25 (with P&W JT9D-1s) – was explored in much more detail. It had a fuselage stretched to 220 feet and a range of 3,500 miles. This was paralleled by a single-deck proposal offering a 585-passenger capacity with a 260-foot fuselage, but the design

Artist's impression of the D-956-13 double decker. Note the first use of the name "DC-10" on the aircraft.

was quickly dropped as being far less efficient than the double-deck concept. The -15/-25 were selected for continued development as both offered seat-mile Direct Operating Costs (DOC) that were 30 percent less than those being predicted for the DC-8-61.

As freighters, the basic -13F/-23F models could carry a space-limited cargo of 215,000 pounds, based on 10 pounds per cubic foot, over 2,775 miles. A typical trans-Atlantic flight of 3,500 miles would have carried a 200,000-pound payload. The stretched versions were not considered for this role.

These studies quietly faded away when Douglas announced in May 1966 the development of a twin-engine "Airbus," intended to replace the Boeing 727-200 and enter service in 1970-71.

Fine dining was proposed for the D-956-13 in 1965. (via Bob Goforth)

Chapter II
THE AIRBUS

The Douglas D-966-1 was the initial response to the Jumbo Twin request from American Airlines. (via Bob Goforth)

Airport runway congestion began to surface as a restriction on traffic growth in 1966 as the introduction of cheaper air fares made possible by the jet-powered transports attracted increasing numbers of passengers. Although aircraft builders were initiating stretched versions of DC-8, DC-9 and Boeing 727, it was becoming apparent that even larger short- and medium-range aircraft would be needed by the end of the decade.

For some time, Frank Kolk, the senior vice president of engineering at American Airlines, had been musing over new specifications for such an airliner to operate high-frequency services over some of American's dense routes, particularly the Chicago-West Coast and New York-Chicago segments. At the same time, a similar design was being considered by many European aircraft manufacturers, with several consortia formed to examine the requirement.

In April 1966, Kolk issued an outline to all of the U.S. manufacturers, including the following criteria:

Airport Operations:
- Same runway footprint as Boeing 727
- Nose-in parking
- Ability to operate from a 7,000-foot runway
- Low noise levels

Size:
- Approximately 250,000 pounds MTOW
- No more than 150 feet in length
- 250-passenger seating capacity with a 36-inch seat pitch

Features:
- Twin-engine
- Low wing
- Minimum Mach 0.82 cruising speed at 31,000 feet
- Range of 1,850 nautical miles – full payload

The primary requirements of this proposal were needed to operate safely from New York City's La Guardia Airport, where the last 2,000 feet of its two runways were built on piers in the Rikers Island channel of Flushing Bay. Nose-in parking was to minimize gate space requirements in the congested ramp areas of La Guardia. The seating capacity and fuselage length limitation effectively created a twin-aisle, widebody configuration.

Aircraft noise levels were becoming a major environmental issue with the New York Port Authority (NYPA), and monitoring systems around its airports resulted in fines for violators. In October 1965, the NYPA wrote to the manufacturers and airlines to warn that operation of new, larger aircraft into New York's airports would be banned if they resulted in noise levels higher than those of the existing DC-8s and Boeing 707s.

Establishing the Basic Design

On receipt of American's request by the Douglas advanced design team, senior configuration layout engineer Richard T. Cathers began examining various fuselage cross-section and cabin length mixes, along with low- and high-wing positioning plus engine locations (under wing or rear positions). Other considerations included single and double decks, nine- versus 10-across seating and circular versus "double bubble" cross-sections. Tradeoff studies of the horizontal stabilizer location were explored, along with the conventional low position, T-tail and even V-tail configurations. The accompanying chart (page 11) gives an idea of some of the various combinations created just between April and July 1966.

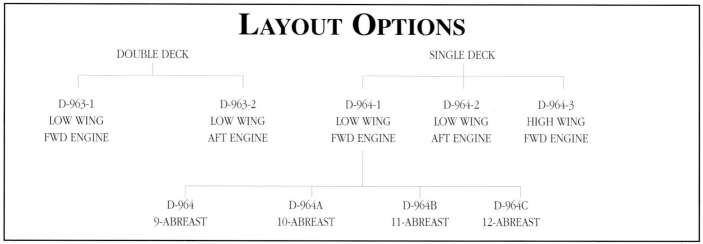

LAYOUT OPTIONS

DOUBLE DECK

D-963-1
LOW WING
FWD ENGINE

D-963-2
LOW WING
AFT ENGINE

SINGLE DECK

D-964-1
LOW WING
FWD ENGINE

D-964-2
LOW WING
AFT ENGINE

D-964-3
HIGH WING
FWD ENGINE

D-964
9-ABREAST

D-964A
10-ABREAST

D-964B
11-ABREAST

D-964C
12-ABREAST

European Airbus

Meanwhile, the concurrent European requirement for a similar aircraft differed from American's need mainly because the range demand was only 750 to 1,000 miles with 250 to 300 seats in a nine-abreast layout. Initially, two Anglo-French groups were formed to study the proposal. British Aircraft Corporation (BAC), Sud Aviation and Avions Marcel Dassault formed the first group, while Hawker Siddeley, Breguet and Nord Aviation created a second alliance to work on a study named the HBN-100. Separately, Arbeitsgemeinschaft Airbus (Airbus Working Group), an all-German consortium led by VFW, also generated a four-engine aircraft proposal.

Later, BAC considered a new version of its Super VC-10 with a reduced wingspan and stretched fuselage that would seat 265 for the role. Sud and Nord, which were about to merge, then decided to join the Airbus Working Group, and the new consortium agreed to use a previously proposed Sud Galion project as a baseline design.

The Galion, first announced in March 1966, was a 241- to 269-seat design with a 20-foot diameter fuselage that measured 147 feet, 8 inches in length with a wingspan of 137 feet, 10 inches. The Galion's MTOW was 210,400 pounds, optimized for a 1,000-mile range.

The HBN-100 was very similar, with both projects tailored to use either the P&W JT9D-1 or Rolls-Royce (RR) RB-178 engine. As a result of the European use of the appellation Airbus, Douglas elected to refer to its new project as the "Jumbo Twin."

Other Opinions

Douglas teams began a series of meetings with other major airlines in June 1966 to get a consensus of requirements. They first met with Norm Parmet and Ed Zak from TWA, who felt that the new airliner's primary requirement would be for transcontinental flights operating from New York's Idlewild Airport, which had no runway limitations. They were also looking for low approach speeds and wanted the aircraft to match the cruising speed of TWA's Convair 880s – Mach 0.85 at 35,000 feet – with noise levels at least 5 to 8 decibels lower than current jets. There was no restriction on weights. Passenger seating was to be 250 in a mixed-class or 300 in an all-economy-class configuration. As an air freighter, TWA required the ability to carry side-by-side, 8-foot by 8-foot containers loaded through the nose. The D-964-1 study showed this capability via a swing nose that included the cockpit. One-stop transcontinental cargo flights were acceptable. Initially, Parmet had no particular preference for the engine manufacturer or number of engines.

Another meeting in June was held with American Airlines officials to review the various Douglas concepts described above. American's Kolk opted for the D-964-1 with its single deck for ease of loading passengers or freight, a low-wing configuration – considered more crash-worthy than high wing – and engines under the wing for a shorter overall length. He also indicated an initial preference for a high cockpit location to be compatible with the Boeing 747.

Meetings were also held with United Air Lines managers who also regarded the New York-Idlewild–Los Angeles route as its primary mission. United had a distinct preference for four smaller engines. Eastern Air Lines was interested in the aircraft for the New York–San Juan route, and as a long-term replacement for DC-8-61s on order at the time.

Competition

While Douglas was completing the many design process refinements, Lockheed had been creating studies for the same mission. Except for participation in the ill-fated SST design competition, its engineers had done little in airliner development since the model 188 Electra program.

By early 1966, Lockheed had established a baseline design referred to as the CL-1011-28, a twin-engine aircraft sized to meet the original American specification. It differed from the Douglas approach by keeping a 19.58-foot diameter fuselage cross-section to a twin-aisle, eight-abreast (2-4-2) layout and did not address TWA's cargo requirements, thus avoiding the need for an upper cockpit location. The Burbank company also looked at three-engine versions, but its designers believed that no financial or performance advantages over its basic design would result from a tri-jet.

Boeing initially remained aloof from any serious effort to go after this market with yet another new aircraft as it was in the throes of designing and producing the first Boeing 747. In addition, the Boeing 737 was due to make its first flight in April 1967 followed by the Boeing 727-200 three months later.

The D-966-1

By August, input from the airlines had been incorporated into a design called the D-966-1 that featured a twin-aisle fuselage 21.16 feet in diameter, capable of 10-abreast (3-4-3) seating for 330 economy-class passengers at a 34-inch pitch, two inches less than the standard tourist-class pitch of 36 inches. A nine-abreast (3-3-3) alternate arrangement reduced total seating to 278. In the all-freighter version, it could carry 23 8-foot by 8-foot by 10-foot containers loaded through the nose. The most noticeable external feature was the high cockpit requested by Frank Kolk. The basic data were:

Span	157.5 feet
Length	175 feet
Height	57 feet
Wing area	3,100 square feet
MTOW	301,500 pounds
MLW	270,800 pounds

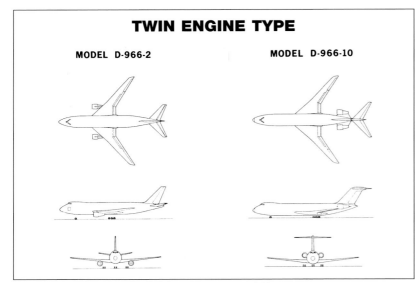

TWIN ENGINE TYPE

MODEL D-966-2   **MODEL D-966-10**

Engines location alternatives for the twin-engine D-966.

The performance quoted was based on a developed P&W JT9D-1 engine, expected to be available in 1972 and capable of 44,000 pounds of thrust. A typical 71,000-pound payload (330 passengers and bags plus 5,000 pounds of cargo) could be carried 1,400 miles with full fuel reserves. A mixed-class version (48 first-class and 197 tourist-class plus baggage and 5,000 pounds of cargo) would reduce range to 2,100 miles. The all-freighter version would lift a 102,000-pound payload over 500 miles.

Trade-Off Studies

A second design, the D-966-2, was powered by the basic JT9D-1 engine rated at 41,000 pounds of thrust, and had a smaller wing area of 2,600 square feet, with a fuselage shortened by 12 feet. This version reduced the all-tourist-class seating to 224 with an MTOW of 279,500 pounds. This design was rapidly followed by D-966-10, identical to the D-966-2 except with rear fuselage-mounted engines and a repositioned wing to maintain the center of gravity (CG).

Yet another spin-off was the D-966-4, with a span of 160 feet, 6 inches; wing area of 3,220 square feet and overall length of 184 feet, 6 inches. It seated 269 in a nine-abreast tourist-class layout or a mixed-class total of 242. All-economy capacity, using DC-8 tourist-class seats at 10-abreast, was 322 passengers. The MTOW was 307,000 pounds. A revised version adopted the wing of the D-966-2 and a shorter fuselage to seat 250 (mixed class) with a reduced MTOW of 286,800 pounds. Although nearly 23,000 pounds heavier than the Lockheed Twin proposal, it offered a 9,000-pound payload increase.

This last version was interesting, as it was the first design that was sized more closely to the then competing Lockheed design that adhered to the 250-seat mixed-class requirement. The wing areas were identical, although the Douglas design had a 37.5-degree sweep at a 25-percent chord versus the L-1011's 32-degree sweep. The Douglas wing also had a thickness-chord ratio of 0.108, compared with Lockheed's 0.09 ratio.

One other major difference in Lockheed's approach was the use of a double-slotted Fowler flap system that extended on tracks before lowering. This was designed to meet the takeoff requirements from La Guardia Airport while keeping the wing areas to a minimum. Douglas used a simple hinged flap with small vanes attached (the basic double slotted flap), similar to all previous Douglas transports going back to the C-74 Globemaster I military transport. Company trade studies of other flap types including Fowler, triple-slotted and similar designs, revealed penalties, including increased tail size, additional cost and reliability concerns.

One other study emerged from the D-966-4, based on a 46,000-pound-thrust engine that allowed an MTOW increase to 329,000 pounds. Carrying

269 economy-class passengers in a nine-abreast seating mode, it would have had transcontinental range, and therefore was dubbed the D-966-TRNS. For study purposes, all of the D-966 models assumed a first cost of approximately $11.6 million in 1967 dollars.

The Team Expands

August also saw the appointment of John Morris as chief of configuration design. His task was to work with the airlines to garner additional input covering both engineering and market aspects. As the studies expanded, James E. Roberts (configuration definition), William M. Douglass (propulsion) and Frederick D. Hess (structures) became involved.

Three years later, on July 1, 1969, Cathers and Morris were jointly awarded U.S. Patent number 214,597 for the basic DC-10 configuration concept. Normally, patents of this nature were issued in the name of the chief designer. All five of the above-mentioned designers were collectively awarded Patent number 3,666,211 for the design of the fin-mounted, rear-engine concept on May 30, 1972. As a side note, Roberts had earlier created at a similar installation when studying a three-engine version of the DC-8 fitted with P&W JT9D-1s.

It has often been said that "fame brings its own rewards." In the case of the DC-10 patent holders, the reward consisted primarily of fame alone. The five patent holders were awarded just $200 to share among themselves for the center engine configuration design. Cathers and Morris were awarded a further $12.50 each for the configuration concept patent. In addition, each received $1 per month during the 14 years that the patents were in effect. By contrast, in December 1972, MDC engineer Gale Sherman was awarded $8,000 for the design of the DC-10 unitized crew seat.

Variations on a Theme

There still was no real consensus among airline managers regarding how many engines would power the new airliner. Douglas engineers, aware that 88,000 pounds thrust was needed to handle all the requirements, began to investigate three- and four-engine versions during the summer of 1966. Several design approaches were generated around a basic specification for a three-engine version powered by an unspecified power plant rated at 29,800 pounds of static thrust. Each of the versions retained a high cockpit and 21.6-foot diameter fuselage.

Two candidates were designated D-967-1 and D-967-10. The fuselage and wing location remained the same as the D-966 -1 and -10 respectively. However, both had T-tail configurations with an "S-duct" center engine inlet similar to that on the Boeing 727. The main difference was that the D-967-10 had all three engines located at the rear, similar to the Boeing 727, while the D-967-1 retained one engine under each wing.

Two more radical three-engine designs were also considered. The most unusual was the D-967-20 that retained two engines under the left wing and a single engine under the right wing at the outboard position. Odd as it sounds, full directional control of the aircraft could be maintained even with the right engine shut down. The D-967-30 mounted two engines on the left rear fuselage, with a single engine on the right side. Loss of any one engine had little effect on control due to the closeness of the engines to the aircraft centerline.

Four-engine designs were also evaluated. The D-968-1 had four 22,000-pound thrust engines mounted under the wings and the D-968-10 had them located VC-10-style, on the rear fuselage. The advantage of four engines over two with the same total thrust was the increased MTOW allowable based on a single engine failure during takeoff.

All of the foregoing designs were also evaluated in trade studies using a conventional cockpit location with a large side door for cargo loading, but at this stage, the nose loading feature remained the primary concept.

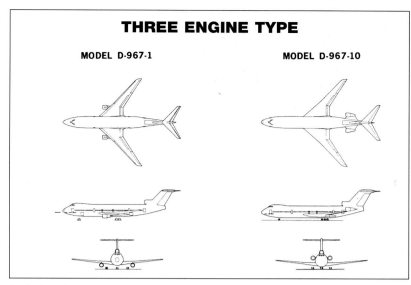

THREE ENGINE TYPE

MODEL D-967-1 **MODEL D-967-10**

Logical engine positions for the proposed D-967 tri-jet.

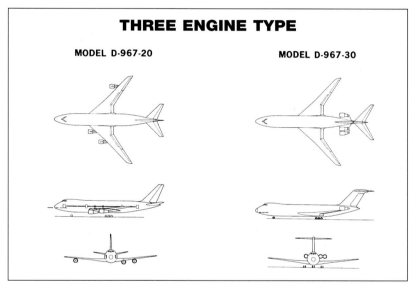

THREE ENGINE TYPE

MODEL D-967-20 **MODEL D-967-30**

More unusual locations examined for the proposed D-967. These positions were viable, even if the solo engine failed.

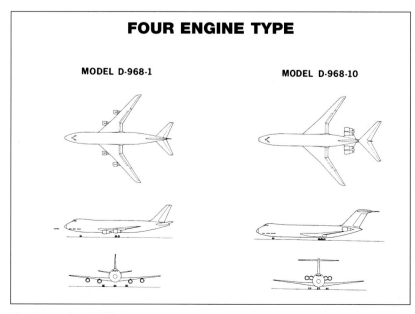

FOUR ENGINE TYPE

MODEL D-968-1 **MODEL D-968-10**

The four-engine D-968 reverted to more traditional locations.

Program Review

In late November 1966, a further round of discussions was held with the major domestic airlines. American's representatives were no longer adamant about the need for a twin-engine design and showed more interest in the cargo version. Oddly, they didn't see the need for an Auxiliary Power Unit. TWA was pushing for three engines, 260 seats and preferred the Rolls-Royce engine to the GE offering. The airline also asked that the Boeing 747's Mach 0.858 cruising speed be matched. Another request was for transcontinental range in case the forthcoming SSTs were limited to subsonic flights across the United States. United's management had split opinions. Its San Francisco engineering team wanted two engines and a 1,850-mile range while the Chicago headquarters staff desired four engines and longer range. Eastern joined TWA in seeking three engines. At a meeting on November 22, 1966, the principal design engineers selected for further investigation the D-966-1 option with the rear engine fed by the "elephant-ear" (bifurcated) intakes and two wing-mounted power plants. Their second choice was the straight-through duct aft the engine mounted behind the elevators. Both had the low horizontal tail surfaces. A third study selected was a T-tailed version with three aft-mounted engines, similar to the Boeing 727 layout. Having chosen these configurations, the next task was to size the vertical fin and rudder in each case.

Simple Solutions

Several other design decisions were addressed at the same time. Initially, the main passenger entry doors were 50 inches wide and 76 inches high. Later, the width was reduced to just 42 inches wide. This decision was the result of a simple but unusual test. Lakewood Boulevard divides the Long Beach plant, with tunnels linking the two factory areas. A large piece of plywood was placed across a pedestrian tunnel with cutouts 32 inches, 42 inches and 50 inches wide to represent three different door sizes. During a shift change, engineers observed how quickly people exited in the usual rush to get to their cars. It was determined that two people easily passed simultaneously through the 42-inch door, so it was adopted for all but the forward aircraft entry. This exercise was important because the fuselage length and resulting passenger capacity dictated how many doors would be required to evacuate the aircraft in 90 seconds with half the exits unavailable.

The goal of achieving the Boeing 727's footprint at La Guardia Airport with two main gear four-wheel bogies became a problem when the MTOW crept above the 300,000-pound mark. Two six-wheel bogies were then proposed for the main landing gear, but this created tire scrubbing and a large turning radius that could only be reduced by utilizing the same expensive and heavy swiveling trailing bogie used on the DC-8. Engineers later created a simpler gear that consisted of a four-wheeled bogie under each wing plus a two-wheeled unit mounted on the aircraft center line. This concept was subsequently adopted for the higher-weight DC-10-30 and -40.

Chapter III
FOCUS CHANGE

A widebody version of the DC-8 powered by four P&W JT9D-1s – designated DC-10-84 – was a stopgap effort to compete with the Boeing 747 by offering the same seat size.

By August 1966, the scope of the design began to change. Previous studies had addressed the original American Airlines requirement for a 250-seat twin-jet to replace the Boeing 727 and provide a domestic cargo aircraft via a common basic design. Contemporary customer thinking was now leaning towards a replacement aircraft for the older Douglas DC-8s, Boeing 707-100s and Boeing 720s. This trend was reflected in the growth of the MTOW and passenger capacity in some of the more recent studies. In addition, market research by Douglas had indicated that a large twin would have limited worldwide sales potential in view of the numerous European efforts to launch a similarly sized Airbus.

Douglas managers had also noticed other trends. Although the original four-engine jets were designed to operate domestic transcontinental services, sales of the lengthened intercontinental P&W-powered Boeing 707-300 and Rolls-Royce equipped Boeing 707-400 far outnumbered the smaller shorter-range models. Likewise, demand for the long-range Douglas DC-8-62s and DC-8-63s had replaced sales of the earlier versions.

This raised yet another concern. In the 1960s, regulations restricted twin-engine aircraft to routings within one hour of a suitable airport during overwater flights. This rule had been established earlier for piston-powered airliners due to engine reliability and was not updated with the advent of jet engines.

One other reason to abandon the twin-engine design was a contemporary International Civil Aviation Organization (ICAO) report showing that 52 percent of the world market operated in stage lengths of less than 1,850 miles. However, increasing the range to 2,500 miles would add another 14 percent of the world's total demand. This was beyond the envisioned capability of the Jumbo Twin at the time.

Family Approach

A design memo to initiate the J-2 (an acronym for Jumbo Twin) plan was issued on August 16, 1966. It requested a review of the D-966-1

systems and performance as this was to be used as a base case for the development of three- and four-engine versions. For a short time, a study designated M-4 was carried out to address United's four-engine aircraft requirement. This aircraft was to have been powered by a developed P&W JT9D-1 engine and differed from the J-2 only in fuselage length and a larger wing area, but shared the same high-lift devices. Both the J-2 and M-4 sizing were to be based on a nine-abreast, 34-inch-pitch seating versus the nine-abreast, 36-inch-pitch configuration of the D-966-1.

Company Problems

While the advanced design group continued the new widebody development, the rest of the Long Beach organization was enduring a wild ride with far-reaching consequences. The first quarter of 1966 proved to be so profitable that management paid off its outstanding revolving credit account, electing to meet its current costs out of cash flow. It could afford to do so because four DC-9s, two DC-8s and several A-4 Skyhawks and other military hardware were being delivered each week. The future looked good because the backlog of aircraft orders from military and commercial sales exceeded $3 billion.

However, things changed dramatically as the second quarter progressed. Expanding military requirements for equipment caused by the buildup in Vietnam started to create many shortages, particularly with engine inventories. This led to aircraft rolling out without power plants, and many parts had to be installed out of position, a costly situation. At the same time, the backlog required hiring and training thousands of unskilled workers. At one point, it was estimated that Douglas was losing $500,000 on each aircraft it delivered. In addition, the first DC-8-61s were still in flight test and due to be joined by the DC-8-62 in August, further increasing a negative cash flow. The company had $170 million in long-term debt and needed a $300 million revolving account to meet day-to-day capital needs.

14

The situation worsened by the end of the third quarter, with losses exceeding $19 million. Management desperately sought new financing, pointing to a rapidly growing DC-9 backlog that would reach 500 airplanes by year end. But the bankers were only willing to advance money provided there were changes in the upper management, which Mr. Douglas would not accept. The outside consultants brought in to help agreed with the bankers and finally proposed that the company seek a merger partner that could inject additional capital and new management.

Five companies made offers and, on January 13, 1967, it was announced that McDonnell Aircraft Company would be the new partner, not a total surprise. Its chairman was James S. McDonnell, known as "Old Mac." He had once been chief design engineer for the Ford Tri-Motor and earlier held a similar position at Hamilton Aviation. Already Douglas Aircraft Company's largest single stockholder, he had always wanted to get back into the business of building airliners. (History was to repeat itself in 1998 when John and James McDonnell became major individual stockholders in Boeing after the Boeing-McDonnell Douglas merger.)

David S. Lewis was brought in as president of the new McDonnell-Douglas Corporation (MDC) and became chairman of the Long Beach division. Donald Douglas Sr. became chairman emeritus of MDC while Donald Douglas Jr. was appointed to the corporate board and remained president of the Douglas Aircraft Division. Old Mac was to take a very active personal interest in the new widebody jet design. Members of the advanced design team made frequent trips to his home in St. Louis, Missouri to keep him up to date.

In concert with the American Airlines requirement study, two other programs were under intense consideration in the advanced design group. A team led by R. E. Pendley was exploring three DC-8 derivatives:

a DC-8 fuselage with a new wing and new engines; a new fuselage fitted to existing wings with new engines; and a three-engine version with new engines. The DC-8 studies were focused on a low-investment program, but none attracted any real airline interest.

The other team led by R. C. Hornburg was developing an all-new commercial cargo transport. Studied in detail, the design also elicited little favor from the airlines. Both of these projects, active until the launch of the DC-10 program, were quietly terminated in mid-1968.

New Designations

By February 1967, the design objectives were formally re-defined to also expand the domestic-range transport into an intercontinental aircraft. This was approached with two "families."

Family 1 was a twin-engine U.S. domestic aircraft powered by engines in the 40,000-pound-thrust class with growth to a three-engine intercontinental model. Family 2 featured a three-engine U.S. domestic aircraft powered by engines in the 30,000-pound-thrust class, with growth to a four-engine intercontinental aircraft.

To differentiate between the long-range and domestic proposals, new identities were introduced in April 1967. From this date forward, the Family 1, D-966, designs would be called J-2 (two engines) and J-3 (three engines). Family 2, the D-967, would include the DC-10-3 (three engines) and DC-10-4 (four engines, later to become the D-968).

Eventually, the required engine-takeoff thrust was increased to 47,000 pounds for Family 2 and 32,000 pounds for Family 1. Unfortunately, there were no production engines available in this latter class until the advent of the Boeing 757 and McDonnell Douglas C-17 many years later. Even so, studies using this thrust level continued in parallel with the JT9D-powered variants.

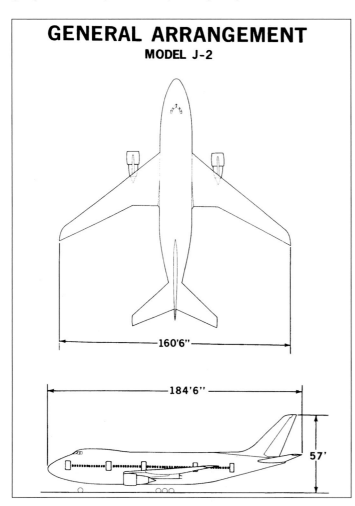

The J-2 version of the D-968 proposal.

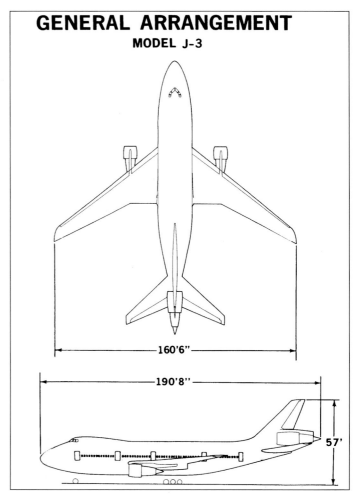

With the addition of the third engine, it was re-designated J-3.

GENERAL ARRANGEMENT
DC-10-3

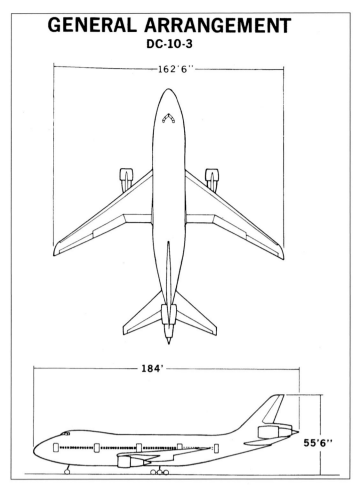

|←——————162'6"——————→|

|←————————184'————————→|

55'6"

The DC-10-3 still retained the bubble cockpit.

GENERAL ARRANGEMENT
DC-10-4

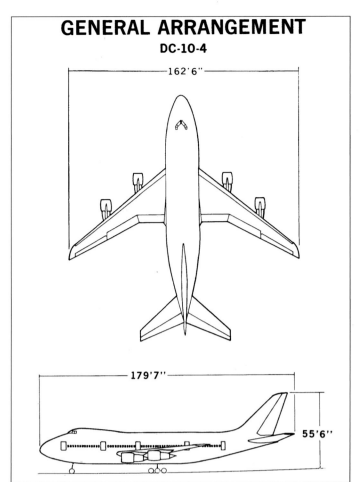

|←——————162'6"——————→|

|←————————179'7"————————→|

55'6"

The four-engine DC-10-4 was aimed primarily at United's requirements.

At this stage, all four designs still retained the upper bubble cockpit and a 23-foot-diameter fuselage, wider than the Boeing 747 that had a floor width of 235 inches and seated nine across (2-4-3) in the tourist configuration. The MDC design retained a floor width of 260 inches, allowing a 10-abreast (3-4-3) arrangement using the same size seat. As a freighter, it could carry an 8-foot by 8.5-foot container with a 125-inch-wide pallet alongside. The belly cargo compartments had 84 inches of headroom versus the Boeing 747's 64-inch clearance.

One additional feature offered to MDC customers was the option to install lower-deck passenger compartments. At a cost of four tourist-class seats on the main deck, 38 seats could be added in a forward lower-deck compartment. With a further reduction in cargo space, a similar compartment aft of the wing box could accommodate another 25 tourist-class seats. Many other alternatives featuring lower-deck lounges were also promoted. The principal galleys were on the main deck, with small galleys to serve the optional lower-deck cabins. However, these choices attracted little enthusiasm due to rapid evacuation or water landing concerns.

The Family 1 and 2 main operating characteristics were as follows:

	J-2	J-3	DC-10-3	DC-10-4
No. of Engines	2	3	3	4
Engine Thrust (pounds)	47,000	47,000	32,000	32,000
MTOW (pounds)	331,100	459,000	334,100	456,400
Operating Weight (pounds)	189,500	224,900	191,300	211,300
All-tourist Seats	298	298	298	298
Mixed Class (15%F/85%T)	264	264	264	264
Range - Mixed-class (miles)	2,600	4,850	2,600	5,200
Takeoff Field Length @ 90°F (ft)	9,800	8,400	6,500	8,700

During a design review, American Airlines representatives indicated that the airline was becoming less interested in the aircraft's cargo carrying capability and preferred the original eight-abreast (2-4-2) seating arrangement which Lockheed had steadfastly maintained. In further meetings with leading potential customers, a consensus was reached that a three-engine version was the optimum design, provided that a suitable power plant could be developed. The configuration offered better high-altitude field performance, better growth potential, lower seat/mile costs, a greater payload/range and a higher return on investment.

Another worry associated with a large twin-jet was the drift-down rate should an engine failure occur while crossing the Rocky Mountains. Because no 30,000-pound-thrust engine appeared to be in sight, the four-engine studies were abandoned in May 1967.

Power Plants

Engines were the key to any further development of widebody tri-jet. Fortunately, three different engines under development promised to meet the requirements for an MDC widebody tri-jet. While Pratt & Whitney developed the JT18D, General Electric was working on the CF6-34, a commercial derivative of the TF-39 engine used on the C-5A. Both were now in the 35,000-pound-thrust class with prototypes operating on test stands. In England, Rolls-Royce had produced the RB.178 advanced turbo-fan demonstration engine. From this, the manufacturer intended to offer a production engine developing 50,000 pounds of thrust. Called the RB.207, it was intended for Lockheed's Twin program. As the focus shifted to a three-engine aircraft, a de-rated "paper" engine design called the RB.211-10 emerged, with a thrust of 34,900 pounds. It was proposed as a baseline engine and, as aircraft weights increased, growth versions would be available. Bench-testing was not expected to start until late 1968. Meanwhile, the RB.204 was proposed. This smaller engine was to be rated at 26,400 pounds of thrust.

The engines varied in length and diameter but MDC had no installation concerns with any of the three since they would be mounted externally. The sizes differed as follows:

	Overall Length	Maximum Diameter
General Electric CF6/34	266 inches	98.8 inches
Pratt & Whitney JT18D	225 inches	95.5 inches
Rolls Royce RB.211-10	218 inches	100 inches

Single Deck Emergence

A re-design to the 2-4-2 seating configuration began to gel in July 1967. The high cockpit was eliminated and the two wing-mounted engines and single rear-engine layout was adopted. By this time, the airlines had considerably downgraded requirements for large cargo volume on this class of aircraft, but retained the priority in the Boeing 747 design, which was battling weight-growth problems. Even TWA softened its need for nose-loading cargo capability on the MDC design, so the swing-nose concept was abandoned too.

The new study, labeled D-967C, was based on using the same seats planned for the Boeing 747. A tourist-class triple-seat unit was 65 inches wide while the double unit measured 44 inches across. The all-economy version with nine-abreast seating utilized seats designed for the DC-9, featuring a 62-inch-wide triple and 44-inch-wide double seat unit. Two parallel studies with different cabin widths were discarded while, during August alone, 11 further studies of different configurations were created. The comparisons differed mainly in fuselage length and minor changes to the wing area and related weights. Two studies were selected for further analysis.

During this design phase, the cockpit profile was finalized. Using the area-rule technique, a smooth transition was created from the nose to the full fuselage circular cross-section. This avoided the high-stress levels experienced in Section 41 of the Boeing 747 that led to fatigue problems in later years. At the same time, the very distinctive cockpit window shapes, based on the military specification proposed for the CX-HLS competition, were designed to give maximum visibility. These efforts resulted in one of the quietest cockpits in a modern jet transport and set a new standard in the crew's field of vision. Spacious accommodation was created for two pilots, a flight engineer and, unusually, two observer seats.

By October, design efforts centered on the rear engine location, with every conceivable alternative reviewed. Using the D-967C-16 derivative design as the baseline aircraft configuration, four different rear engine locations were chosen for further exploration:

Case A - Long inlet
Case B - S-bend inlet
Case C1 - Mounted forward of the vertical tail
Case A1 - Buried aft of the vertical tail.

Case C1 was suggested by Old Mac himself, no doubt based on his jet fighter design background, but was quietly discarded simply because of the inherent danger of shrapnel from an exploding engine penetrating the pressurized passenger cabin.

A number of common factors were examined, including weight, performance, noise, structural complexity, maintenance, the thrust reverser, commonality with the wing engine, potential for growth and development problems. The rear engine location also affected the size of the vertical tail and eventually led to a double-hinged rudder for maximum control. The overall height was constrained by existing hangar-door dimensions. Designers also looked at ways to avoid shrapnel damage to the horizontal stabilizer in the event of a catastrophic engine failure.

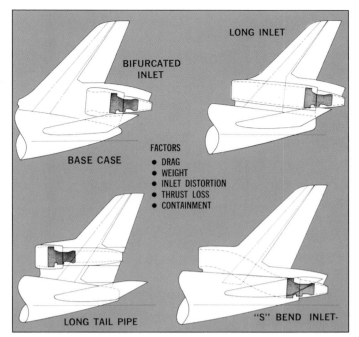

The final rear engine locations considered. One T-tail version mimicked the boundary layer intake of the Boeing 747-300 but was rejected due to the risk of ingesting debris.

Although it was quickly established that a rear-mounted engine was preferred, the air intake design proved to be another major exercise. Preliminary wind tunnel tests showed that bifurcated intakes on both sides of the fin provided the best configuration.

This design, called the D-967-20, was generated by engineers who had worked on the Douglas A-4 Skyhawk that also had bifurcated inlets leading to a single engine. The S-bend intake was rejected as tunnel tests showed inefficiencies caused by friction and loss of pressure from the longer duct and a deep boundary layer within the ducting.

The Configuration Hardens

As the pace quickened, more than 400 people were assigned to the program. A key figure was Harold W. Adams, who was appointed chief engineer. Adams earlier held a similar position on the DC-9 program and was instrumental in organizing the systems designs and related trade studies organization. Much of the success of the DC-10's short development span – just 26 months from launch to first flight – was due to his leadership.

Airline sales talks intensified, though no orders were expected before the end of 1967. MDC marketing managers felt that there was a huge market – 900 total by 1980 – for aircraft in this category. Indeed, Lockheed's forecast was for around 1,000 aircraft. Numerous cabin mock-ups were built and wind tunnel testing increased. Because of the recent DC-8 and DC-9 delivery problems, major efforts were directed at facilities planning, including a new assembly building and an engineering test center. The purchasing of long-lead items and preliminary negotiations for sub-contracting various portions of the aircraft were also initiated.

The DC-10A

The D-967-20 became the known as the DC-10A in October, with a longer, heavier version, the DC-10B, identified as an alternative model. American's specification originally called for a Mach 0.82 cruising speed, but MDC decided that the Mach 0.85 cruise speed requested for the transcontinental case was realistic with minimal penalties. Both models featured the same wing with an area of 3,550 square feet; wing sweep was 35 degrees at 25 percent chord, with an aspect ratio of 6.8 to 1. The

Artist's impression of the DC-10B. This design was longer than the final version.

DC-10B had a slightly smaller horizontal tail due to the longer fuselage. Other differences are listed below.

	DC-10A	DC-10B
Length (feet)	170.00	191.00
Span (feet)	155.33	155.33
Height (feet)	55.75	55.75
MTOW (pounds)	342,200	383,000
Maximum Landing Weight (pounds)	308,000	344,700
Operating Empty Weight (pounds)	195,455	213,420
Takeoff Field Length (feet)	6,100	9,330
Range (nautical miles)	2,500	1,980
Payload (pounds)	51,000	75,580
Seating (Economy) 34-inch pitch; 9-abreast	299	345
Cargo volume (cubic feet)	2,637	3,680
Fuel Capacity (pounds)	147,400	147,400

At this stage, a large lower galley was introduced, positioned under a main deck galley used mainly for food distribution. The idea was to get the kitchen aspect away from the passenger and also to allow cart loading through a galley access door on the left side without impeding passenger boarding. Twelve food carts were loaded individually. A staircase provided access to the lower galley while carts were sent to the upper galley via a double-elevator system.

Approval for further design and development was given at a meeting of the McDonnell Douglas Board of Directors on November 1, 1967, even though no firm orders had yet been received. Production would not be authorized until firm orders were received.

Boeing Re-Enters the Fray

By now, Boeing was becoming concerned that the improved-range DC-10/L-1011 specifications were creating an aircraft that could eat into the lower end of its Boeing 747 market. The Seattle designers began investigating a tri-jet version of the Boeing 747-100, to be appropriately designated as the Boeing 747-300.

This simple mock-up was used early in the program to sell Old Mac the DC-10 concept. (via Gerry Kingsley)

The Boeing 747-300

To compete in the transcontinental market with a 250-seat mixed-class, widebody aircraft, Boeing offered a shortened model of the Boeing 747-100. As with the MDC and Lockheed designs, the required engine thrust and available engines dictated that the new aircraft would be a tri-jet.

Though designers were able to utilize most of the Boeing 747 fuselage, a new, smaller wing spanning 159 feet, 6 inches (versus 195 feet) was introduced. Total wing area was reduced to 4,000 square feet compared to its big brother's 5,500 square feet. A high degree of 747-100 systems, cockpit, engines and spares commonality was maintained to attract the existing customers.

Establishing a third engine installation required a completely new rear fuselage and empennage design. Various engine air intake options were examined, including the unusual "boundary layer" intake, a shallow scoop extending around most of the rear fuselage. MDC designers had also examined this concept, but quickly abandoned it due to the danger of debris being sucked up from the ground. Other intakes included straight-through and S-bend configurations. Low-set horizontal stabilizers, T-tails and numerous fuselage lengths were also considered. The final versions were established by April 1968.

The main landing gear was totally redesigned to help spread the footprint for the La Guardia Airport case. Two four-wheeled units were located inboard of the engines, retracting into the fuselage. Two double-wheeled bogies mounted under the fuselage retracted forward and rotated for stowage in the fuselage.

The last two models offered to the airlines were the Dash 305B with the low-set tail and the Dash 306B with the T-tail layout. The Dash 306B proved the most promising design. A cargo version (with an upward-hinging nose) of this configuration was later adopted for Boeing 747F models. Seating arrangements included 51 first-class seats (2-2-2) at a 38-inch pitch, plus 180 tourist-class seats at a 36-inch pitch on the main deck (2-2-2-2) and 44 more on the upper deck (2-2-1), for a total of 275 passengers. A 298-seat version offered the same first-class layout with 201 tourist-class seats – nine-across (2-2-2-3) – on the main deck, plus 41 seats on the upper deck (2-2-1), all at a 34-inch pitch.

The target performance was a 2,750-mile range with 275 passengers and baggage plus 5,000 pounds of cargo. The all cargo-version carried a 75,000-pound payload over 2,200 miles. These figures were based on an MTOW of 440,000 pounds and Operational Empty Weight (OEW) of 261,000 pounds. The engines were three P&W JT9D-3s (43,500-pound thrust) or JT9D-7s (45,500-pound thrust).

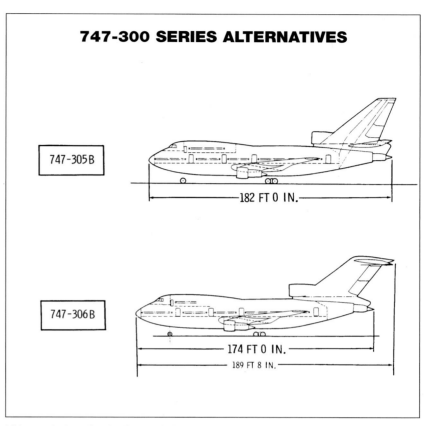

747-300 SERIES ALTERNATIVES

747-305B

├─ 182 FT 0 IN. ─┤

747-306B

├─ 174 FT 0 IN. ─┤
├── 189 FT 8 IN. ──┤

Ultimate designs for the Boeing 747-300 proposal. (Boeing-Seattle Archives)

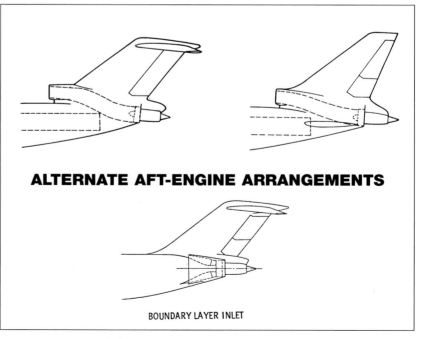

ALTERNATE AFT-ENGINE ARRANGEMENTS

BOUNDARY LAYER INLET

Alternate Boeing 747-300 rear engine arrangements. (Boeing-Seattle Archives)

Chapter IV
THE LAUNCH BATTLE

This was the first picture to be released showing the final engine locations. It was used to announce the initial American order.

The forthcoming sales campaigns were to be like nothing seen before in the aircraft manufacturing industry. Throughout the years, most airliner sales had depended closely on personal relationships established between the pioneers and entrepreneurs of both the airline and manufacturing industries. But now, Donald Douglas and most of his counterparts in the airlines were gone. United's William Patterson and Eddie Rickenbacker of Eastern had retired and C. E. Woolman of Delta had passed away, leaving just American's C. R. Smith and Robert F. Six of Continental from the old fraternity. Transactions now would become more businesslike events based on buyer and seller team interface on a large scale.

As 1968 began, the sales battle intensified as the aircraft and engine manufacturers placed increasing pressure on the airline managers to make a decision. Most of the MDC negotiating was done by David S. Lewis, assisted by Jackson R. McGowen – senior vice president in charge of all aircraft operations at Long Beach – and John Brizendine, the vice president of engineering. Teams of salesmen, sales engineers, customer engineers, market research personnel, financial analysts and product support specialists all worked with their airline counterparts to ensure that the maximum information was available to the airlines. Central to MDC's effort was establishing a final fuselage length and its weight-related payload/range performance.

Financing

Prior to the merger, McDonnell Aircraft Company had been debt-free with ample cash reserves to enjoy a positive cash flow from increasing F-4 Phantom sales. Profits from the Long Beach division returned as DC-9 production was brought back on schedule and DC-8 deliveries accelerated. Although it was planned to deliver some 180 DC-9s and 90 DC-8s during the year, MDC delivered more than 200 DC-9s and 101

DC-8s by year's end. Even so, corporate financial managers sought the additional $250 million needed to launch a new program of the DC-10's magnitude. More than $1 billion would be needed to fund the program that was expected to turn profitable once between 250 and 300 aircraft were sold. To achieve this, orders would have to reach between $3.8 billion and $4.5 billion.

Final Rear Engine Position

Even though the bifurcated intakes had been selected as the primary rear engine design, it was later discovered that the airflow was unbalanced when the aircraft was in a yaw attitude. Changing to a straight-through duct eliminated this situation but created an engineering challenge to build the fin structure around the duct while keeping its weight to a minimum. This was finally resolved by sculpting four spars (henceforth known as "Banjo" fittings) from huge aluminum forgings using computer-controlled machines. The finished spars measured 210 inches long and 110 inches in diameter where the duct casing passed through it. The finished fittings had a maximum thickness of eight inches.

When all the tradeoff studies were assessed, it was shown that the straight duct improved engine cruise thrust by 5.2 percent. The change also produced a 900-pound weight reduction, minimized airflow distortion and required less engine noise suppression material. The latter was significant because MDC had incurred a weight penalty of 3,000 pounds in sound suppression material in order to meet noise guarantees. Specific fuel consumption showed a 3.8 percent improvement over the S-duct configuration.

On September 11, 1967, Lockheed got the jump on MDC by announcing that it would accept orders for the L-1011 – to be named "TriStar" – and would commit to production as soon as sufficient contracts were signed. Airline buyers found little to choose between the two contenders. In general, most engineering staffs leaned slightly towards the TriStar whereas corporate managers preferred the long, unbroken tradition of Douglas commercial aircraft.

At American, President C. R. Smith was in favor of the TriStar-Rolls-Royce combination, but he suddenly resigned from the airline in order to take a Cabinet post as Secretary of Commerce. His replacement, George Spater, was much more in favor of MDC because of the company's reputation. All of the other senior executives, including Kolk, agreed with him. Additionally, American's relationship with Lockheed had been less than smooth during earlier turboprop Electra problems.

American's managers all preferred the RB.211 engine for the DC-10. This was based on their experience with the Rolls-Royce Spey engine that powered their BAC 1-11 fleet and the personal relationships between American and Rolls-Royce senior managers. In addition, the cost of the RB.211 had been reduced via a five percent devaluation of the British pound against the U.S. dollar on October 18, 1967.

To remain competitive with Lockheed, MDC announced on January 29, 1968, that it would launch the DC-10 on receipt of sufficient orders. There was additional apprehension that delaying a start commitment would allow Boeing to catch up with the Boeing 757, a totally new design about which little was known. Boeing made no announcements concerning its Dash 300 at the time.

American's Decision

On February 19, 1968, the MDC and Lockheed sales team leaders were invited to hear American's decision. George Spater told David Lewis and his MDC associates that they had won while the Lockheed team, led by Lockheed's president Dan Houghton, waited in an outer office. The American order was for 25 firm and 25 options plus spares with deliveries beginning in late 1971, a contract valued at more than $800 million if the options were picked up. By mutual agreement, the deal was not to be considered firm unless two other airlines placed orders within 90 days. The actual aircraft price was about $16 million per airplane. American declined to specify which engine would equip the DC-10, astutely aware of impending political problems.

At the beginning of March, Representative Robert Taft Jr. made a speech to Congress concerning the possible loss of jobs in his Ohio congressional district where GE's main engine manufacturing facilities were located. Senator Frank J. Lausche, also of Ohio, wrote a letter to the White House expressing similar concerns. These moves were in response to reports that the U.S. Treasury Department would approve dollar exports to pay for the imported RB.211 engine.

Lockheed's Response

Lockheed reacted very quickly to its loss and made revised offers to TWA and Eastern, reducing the price from the $17 million-plus bid price offered to American to less than $15 million per aircraft. On March 29, the two airlines jointly ordered 94 TriStars powered by RB.211s. In addition, little-known British company Air Holdings Ltd. announced that it had ordered 30 TriStars plus 20 options, for re-sale outside the United States. This latter order was the Lockheed and Rolls-Royce strategy to counter rising political opposition to the use of a foreign engine in an aircraft primarily destined for the American domestic market.

In essence, Air Holdings Ltd. had obtained guaranteed line positions with no particular customers in view. At the time, the company was simply a financial group that did not even have a sales executive. The agreement stipulated that any foreign airline sales completed by Lockheed would be deducted from Air Holdings' commitment. Should Lockheed sell 50 aircraft abroad, the Air Holdings agreement would be nullified.

Afraid that the DC-10 might not go into production, Delta purchased 24 TriStars in April 1968 although its engineering department wanted the GE CF6-34 engine. Lockheed had initially offered both the GE and Rolls-Royce engine, but dropped the choice after the Air Holdings agreement was consummated. Another order for four TriStars came from Northeast Airlines, which later merged with Delta before taking delivery.

MDC and American were in a precarious position because three major airlines had opted for the TriStar, putting Lockheed in a position to go ahead with production and Rolls-Royce order books left little room for early engines for American Airlines' DC-10s. Should MDC fail to launch, American would have little option but to join the end of the line at Lockheed since all the early delivery positions were now reserved.

United executives were ambivalent regarding airframe selection, but leaned heavily towards the GE engine even though it was more expensive than the RB.211-15 price tag of $540,000 per unit. They pressed Lockheed for the TriStar equipped with GE engines too, but didn't get a favorable response. United's second choice was the P&W JT9D-powered Boeing 747-300 which had drawn little interest from anyone else.

Faced with this situation, MDC and GE put together a package that brought the CF6-34-powered DC-10 price down to match the Lockheed-Rolls-Royce offer.

An Improved Wing

While the campaign to win United continued, MDC engineers working with American's latest inputs, made a number of changes to the DC-10 design. First, the straight through rear-engine inlet was finally adopted on March 1, 1968. The fuselage length was also set at 181 feet, 7 inches, with a diameter of 19.75 feet, giving American a mixed-class capacity of 46 first-class, six-abreast seating at a 38-inch pitch, plus 208 in tourist-class, configured at eight across (2-4-2) with a 36-inch pitch. The two middle tourist seats had an 8-inch-wide table between the arm rests to create a spacious atmosphere. The DC-10's overall height was established at 57 feet, 3 inches.

A more critical but less obvious change was made to the wing design. Although the wing retained its basic shape and span, the taper ratio was changed slightly to 0.30. This increased the chord at the wing tip, leading to the possibility of extending the tip when heavier, intercontinental models were introduced. The sweep at 25 percent chord remained at 35 degrees and the thickness/chord ratio remained at about 11 percent. However, the aerodynamic twist in the wing was modified to improve overall performance characteristics. Increasing the twist improved the longitudinal pitching moments beyond buffet onset. These changes were optimized for a low stall speed of less than 100 knots, and minimum field requirements while retaining a Mach 0.85 cruise speed, although the airplane could cruise at Mach 0.88 with a slight fuel flow penalty. Normal long-range-cruise speed was Mach 0.82.

The wing-pylon-nacelle combination worked well in the wind tunnel and required little tweaking. The leading-edge slat configuration was similar to that used on the DC-9 Series 30, except that the slats were either fully extended for landing or at an intermediate setting for takeoff. The DC-9 had a single, extended setting to meet both configurations.

However, slow-speed wind tunnel tests showed that, with slats extended, the large engine nacelle position close to the wing leading edge and the pylon, along with the nacelle and leading-edge junction, combined to create a flow disturbance that caused premature stalling of the wing immediately behind the nacelle. This condition led to the introduction of the two strakes mounted on the upper shoulders of the wing engine nacelles. The modification generated a strong leading-edge vortex at high angles of attack that went directly over the wing just behind the nacelle and energized the wing airflow sufficiently to eliminate the stalling problem.

While initial test flights were made without the strakes, various sizes were later evaluated, leading to a production version that increased the maximum lift coefficient by more than 10 percent, reducing stall speeds and improving takeoff and landing performance. Strakes were subsequently used by both Boeing and Airbus Industries on some aircraft using large diameter pylon-mounted engines, and also appeared on the DC-8-70 series power plants.

Final DC-10-10 Design and Launch

At this stage, the DC-10's MTOW had risen to 410,000 pounds with GE's CF6-34 engines rated at 35,600 pounds of thrust. The design was still able to meet the runway strength criteria at La Guardia Airport because, with a full passenger load plus 5,000 pounds of cargo, the aircraft could operate the La Guardia-to-Chicago mission with an MTOW of just 330,000 pounds. A long stroke piston in the landing gear struts and the wide wheel spacing on each bogie created acceptable runway loading limits.

The combination of these changes was subsequently incorporated in Model D-967C-33, which formally became the DC-10-10 on June 21, 1968, after the GE CF6-36 with 39,500 pounds of thrust had been chosen as the primary engine.

United president George Keck announced the purchase of 30 GE-powered DC-10s plus 30 options, on April 25. The firm order was valued at $465 million including engines and spares. Aircraft were approximately $15.5 million each including engines. Old Mac immediately announced a "full speed ahead" commitment to build the aircraft. MDC also indicated that initial deliveries to American and United would be made simultaneously in August 1971. Keck stated that overall contractual terms had been the major consideration in making the purchase although there were also concerns as to whether Rolls-Royce could develop its engine on schedule.

The next move was an MDC and GE meeting with American and United to convince American to accept the CF6-36. The price offered to American was also adjusted to match the United price, as the aircraft were virtually identical. The only differences were the interior decor and the external markings. Follow-on customers would be allowed minimal latitude in deviating from this specification, particularly on the flight deck.

MDC stock trading on the New York Stock Exchange was temporarily halted because of the rush of buyers. When trading resumed, the stock had jumped considerably and was the most actively traded on that day. A similar reaction was witnessed on the Pacific Coast Stock Exchange. At the same time, Boeing announced the abandonment of the Boeing 747-300 tri-jet in order to concentrate on developing a smaller aircraft. Pratt & Whitney appeared to be out of the large tri-jet competition. The main reason the JT9D was rejected by American and United was that the engine was considerably heavier than either of its competitors.

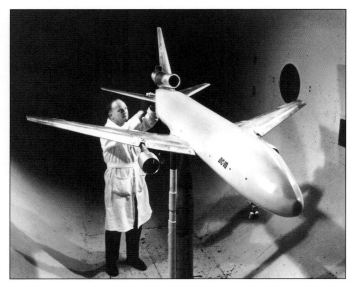

A 4.7-percent scale model of the DC-10 shown undergoing tests in the NASA Ames wind tunnel at Moffett Field, California.

During this intense period, the U.S. Air Force had been seeking proposals for two aircraft to replace the early 707 aircraft used for presidential travel. MDC had been offering a suitably modified version of the DC-8-62 to compete with the Boeing 707-320B. With the drastic reduction in price of the DC-10 to the airlines, two DC-10-10s were offered for a base price of approximately $16 million each. However, lack of sufficient available funding precluded the purchase.

Gearing Up

A number of management changes were instituted at the beginning of May. John Brizendine was appointed vice president and general manager of the DC-10 program with William T. Gross as his deputy. Clifford L. Stout became DC-10 project pilot. Previously, he had been in charge of developing all-weather flight systems, including the heads-up display on the DC-8 and DC-9.

A tight schedule was set, with the first rollout slated for July 1970 and first flight two months later. The certification program was to be completed in 13 months using five aircraft; FAA certification was targeted for October 1971. This would require 1,050 hours of flight testing for development and evaluation plus 300 hours for FAA certification flying and 150 hours for FAA functional and reliability proving.

Production plans called for delivery of 12 aircraft by the end of 1971 and a total of 93 by the end of 1973. To reach these goals, new construction was authorized to add a 600,000-square foot assembly hall, a similarly sized parts storage unit plus a 250,000-square foot engineering research facility capable of housing a DC-10.

By July, 1,270 engineers were assigned to the program and 3,000 hours of wind tunnel work was completed. By the time the DC-10 first flew, tunnel testing would total 12,000 hours, utilizing 22 different models. A full size fuselage mock-up was used to develop the interior and its associated furnishings. A separate cockpit mock-up was kept in constant use while the ideal instrument layout was designed with input from visiting airline pilots. For the first time, a human factors group was set up to make all aspects of the aircraft "livable."

The new buzz word was "ergonomics." In all, some 16 different mock-ups were assembled. Later in the development cycle, others would be added when new interior design concepts were introduced. In August, detail design of the entire outer wing was assigned to engineers at St. Louis.

Construction also began on a full size "Iron Bird" skeletal airframe, used to test-fit all the plumbing, wiring and associated fittings before the components were committed to production. Other smaller mock-ups supplemented the Iron Bird in specific areas such as the pylons and the hydraulics bay, universally referred to as the "hell hole." This approach saved a substantial amount of money and time over the old method of simply fitting items into a production aircraft.

A second Iron Bird was constructed in the new research facility to develop the flight control systems. It included a cockpit, all the wing and tail control surfaces plus associated hydraulic, mechanical and electrical systems. Connected to a computer, this device also acted as a flight simulator to provide data on control characteristics and their dynamic responses.

To assist in structural testing of skin panels, structure and wing-to-fuselage joints, MDC engineers designed and built four large fatigue test machines. Each unit could apply loads up to 1.5 million pounds at a 15-cycle-per-second rate to test pieces as big as 8 feet by 18.5 feet. Later, three test rigs were set up to subject components to loads simulating 84,000 flights and 120,000 hours flight time. These comprised the cockpit section, the rear empennage section and the center fuselage component including the wings. The landing gear was put through separate testing equivalent to 100,000 landings.

Components of the test airframe brought together for a family portrait before being individually tested to destruction.

Subcontracts

Twenty-five percent of the subassembly construction was contracted out to spread the manufacturing burden. Each of the major sub-contractors self-funded the design and manufacture of its work, similar to the cost-profit sharing scheme pioneered on the DC-9 program. Another 25 percent of the work was allocated to MDC facilities located outside of Southern California, such as the Malton, Ontario plant that MDC was in the process of purchasing from de Havilland Aircraft of Canada. It had been decided to invest a considerable sum at that location in the form of computer-controlled milling machines to produce the large tapered spar caps and assemble the two wing halves. The Canadian facility had been producing all the wings and empennages for the DC-9 series plus DC-8 floor sections.

The first of many major subcontracts was signed in August with Rohr Corporation, which would produce the engine pods. General Dynamics agreed to build all five of the fuselage barrel sections at San Diego, with two forward upper and lower sections and two similar aft sections mated prior to shipment to Long Beach. The fifth unit was an upper segment that fitted over the wing box. Much of the barrel design work was assigned to Convair engineers who commuted daily from San Diego to Long Beach on a Convair 240.

The MDC Santa Monica plant was awarded cockpit section production, although years later it was transferred to Long Beach when the Santa Monica facility was closed. Other MDC plants in California, Missouri and Oklahoma produced control surfaces and the wing leading edge. The wing carry-through structure and the aft fuselage with its center-engine mounting structure – both too large to transport – were built at Long Beach. Ling-Temco-Vought (LTV) was awarded the horizontal tail construction while the fin plus fuselage skin panels were to be built in

Italy by AerFer, a major supplier of DC-9 skin panels. AerFer was subsequently contracted to provide the fins and rudders. The only component to be dual-sourced was the nose landing gear, with contracts awarded to Dowty in the United Kingdom and Abex Industries in Canada. Howmet, a long-time Douglas supplier, manufactured the main landing gear in California.

DC-10 final assembly would be located in Building 84, home of the joint DC-9 and DC-8 production lines. The DC-9 line would be transferred to a building with a lower ceiling. DC-10 finishing work (installation of interiors, customer inspections and similar tasks) would be completed in the new building to be located across the airport, away from the existing complex.

Thinking Ahead

Even at this early juncture, GE and MDC were beginning to plan for growth versions of the DC-10. The initial CF6-36 engines would be certified by July 1970, with an increase in thrust to 43,000 pounds by July 1972 and 45,000 pounds by June 1975. The engine air-intake diameters were all sized to accommodate the increased airflow required by developed CF6 engines.

Recent changes to the wing allowed an increased MTOW to approximately 500,000 pounds with only minor modifications. Inclusion of the provision for a centerline landing gear would keep runway flotation pressures within limits at the higher weight. The center section had ample room for additional fuel. Work also continued on long-range DC-10 proposals. In addition, consideration was given to versions stretched up to 55 feet and capable of seating 409 passengers in mixed-class layouts. These proposals were contingent upon the promised growth in engine capability.

Workers give scale to the DC-10's rear engine installation.

Fuselauge barrels under construction at the Convair Division of General Dynamics, San Diego.

Back to Basics

Now that the DC-10 general configuration had evolved, the advanced design group took a step back. Trying to maximize the design, they again looked at a twin-engine design, adopting the designation D-969C. This essentially utilized the DC-10 airframe with a reduced-length fuselage and a new tail without a center engine. It carried approximately 236 passengers in mixed-class seating with a lower deck galley similar to the basic DC-10. The twin design was to go through many modifications over the next several years.

Direct Lift Control

A series of test flights carried out during the summer of 1968 with a DC-8-63 were intended to have a direct impact on the DC-10's low-speed handling. Forty-three approaches and landings were carried out with three of the five spoilers on each wing rigged to operate in response to elevator inputs. Maneuvers were also flown without the spoilers interconnected during approach and landing for comparison. The test results were positive, and the system was installed on the first few DC-10s and retained throughout the FAA certification program. However, the aircraft performed just as well without them. Subsequent auto-land test flying also showed that the system, referred to as Direct Lift Control, was not necessary, so it was removed to save weight and cost.

Custom artwork was created for every sales brochure. The same artist, using an airbrush on a photo of Ship One, completed most renderings.

Northwest Airlines was the next potential DC-10 customer, but its managers were looking for greater payload and range capability needed on the company's trans-Pacific routes. Northwest president Donald W. Nyrop insisted that the engine be compatible with Northwest's Boeing 747 fleet. He is reported to have said, "If I want a light bulb, I'll go to GE; if I want an engine, I'll go to Pratt & Whitney." Northwest had never used any other manufacturer's engines, dating back to the DC-3. The desired variant was Pratt & Whitney's JT9D-15 which was rated at 45,000 pounds. It was identical to the 747's JT9D-7 power plant except that all the engine accessories were mounted on the fan housing rather than the core; all rotating parts and most of the fixed items were interchangeable.

Introduction of the JT9D-15 on the DC-10 required slightly larger engine pods and a modified center engine inlet shape. The engine diameter was a few inches greater than the CF6-10 for which the center engine's duct cross-section was sized. The GE engine was positioned right up to the center engine inlet duct, whereas the JT9D-15 had to be moved 20 inches aft with defuser section added. The inlet duct also was slightly increased in diameter to handle the 15 percent increase in required airflow, giving this version the noticeably bulbous center engine intake.

Initially, the long-range DC-10's MTOW was increased to 490,000 pounds and the fuel capacity rose to 220,000 pounds, providing a 4,200-mile range. The additional fuel capacity was gained by activating the center fuel tank. The higher gross weight led to the introduction of the centerline main landing gear slightly aft of the wing-mounted units. Forward-thinking designers provided parallel twin keel beams rather than the traditional single-beam configuration on the aircraft centerline. This left space between the two beams for the new landing gear. At the higher operating weight, the DC-10 could operate from the same runway thickness (12.2 inches of concrete) as the DC-8-55. An additional 0.7 inch concrete thickness would permit up to 550,000 pounds MTOW with the same runway loading as a DC-8-63.

Long-range DC-10 Launch

On October 30, 1968, Northwest's Nyrop announced the purchase of 14 DC-10s plus 14 options, with deliveries scheduled to commence in January 1973. The price was $14.9 million each, including the more powerful engine and increased capabilities.

Naturally, MDC looked to its traditional customers overseas to replace their DC-8 fleets with DC-10s. The first airlines to be targeted were KLM, SAS and Swissair, which had formed a group known as KSS (UTA joined later and the group was re-named KSSU) to achieve a mutually agreed-upon cockpit configuration and engine selection. The carriers already shared DC-8 fleet maintenance tasks with each airline specializing in the overhaul of specific parts and systems.

Initial MDC offers were for the same aircraft configuration selected by Northwest, except that a choice of engine was offered, either the JT9D-15 or an upgraded GE CF6-10 model; both were rated at 45,600 pounds of thrust. For an introductory period, GE planned to rate the first few production engines at 43,600 pounds while operating experience was built up. This plan restricted the MTOW to 475,000 pounds. Interestingly, MDC applied the same design designation, D-967C-37, to the long-range model, regardless of engine selection.

New Lower Galleys

After a review by American and United, it was decided to totally re-design the lower galley complex. Originally, the unit had been located aft of the Number Two door with carts loaded directly into the galley through a separate access door. The revised location put the new galley directly under the first-class compartment. An elevator that could transport people or food carts replaced the spiral staircase. An adjacent elevator carried only carts. Eight cart modules, containing four food or beverage carts each, would now be loaded through the forward cargo hatch, then

The original lower galley mock-up for the DC-10A/B.

View looking aft in the production lower galley.

The author (white-shirted on left) watches reconfiguration of the original DC-10 mock-up. The forward section was being replaced with a new unit holding the new lower galley.

through doors on either side of the elevator bank and locked into place on a tracked system. Modules for waste and other service items were also added. A bank of high-performance ovens was mounted above the modules on one side of the galley and an emergency exit ladder was installed at the forward end of the galley. To test this layout, a major rebuild of the mock-up – equipped with prototype elevators – was undertaken in mid-1968.

Lockheed retained the method of loading single carts directly into the lower galley through a small access door. In a series of patent rights disputes between Lockheed and MDC, the U.S. Patent Office granted the patent for the original lower galley concept to Lockheed and issued the previously mentioned aircraft configuration and center engine patents to MDC.

Developing In-flight Catering

One of the problems of introducing aircraft of this size onto short sectors was the ability to offer a full meal and drink service to 250 passengers. To ensure it could be done, MDC modified the new mock-up with a complete set of working ovens. A team of airline flight attendants worked with MDC staff to develop the meal service. On November 11, after a few dry runs using MDC personnel, 250 invited airline managers were offered a full bar and hot meal service utilizing the lower galley. Among the guests were several Boeing representatives because the airlines wanted the service system to be compatible with the Boeing 747 while using standard carts, ovens and other equipment. Typical first- and coach-class service was provided in the relevant cabins. To ensure realistic timing, passengers in the coach section were issued script in various denominations to purchase their drinks. From start to cleanup took just 67 minutes. The same trial was also used to time the boarding of passengers, all of whom had been issued boarding passes with seat assignments. Closed-circuit video cameras were used to record the exercise. Initially, it had been planned that two flight attendants would be stationed in the lower galley, but the tests demonstrated that only one was required. The second crew member was re-located upstairs to control the cart flow in the galley area.

Evacuation Tests

A critical part of the mock-up program took place in August 1968. Verification of the exit door sizes was undertaken to establish how many passengers could be evacuated in 90 seconds with half of the exits blocked. For some time, a small team of employee volunteers had taken part in testing different evacuation slide systems and the best way to use them. One drill ended in disaster when a chute side cushion collapsed, pitching several of the team into a pile on the floor; several were injured. It was determined that a diamond ring worn by someone was probably responsible for puncturing the slide. A full scale evacuation of 354 passengers and crew left the mock-up via four exits in 76 seconds. The flight attendants were supplied by DC-10 customer airlines. The mix of passengers included children and senior citizens in FAA-mandated proportions.

Aircraft Model Nomenclature

On November 25, a formal notice was issued to differentiate between the three models on offer:

Series	Specification	Configuration
10	DTS-5300	Domestic, General Electric Engines
20	DTS-5450	Long Range, Pratt & Whitney Engines
30	DTS-5400	Long Range, General Electric Engines.

Henceforth, American and United aircraft would be known as DC-10-10s and Northwest's variant became the DC-10-20.

Also on November 25, Glenn Kramer, the President of Trans International Airlines (TIA), announced an order for three long-range DC-10s plus three DC-8-63CFs. TIA, a major U.S. supplemental carrier, did not specify the DC-10 engine type in its initial announcement, nor was any mention made about a convertible model. The airline had 90 days to select the engine type.

Manufacturing

Formal production was initiated on January 6, 1969, at the MDC Torrance, California facility when the first cuts were made on the windshield forging. Ten days later, milling of the first of the 80-foot-long wing spar caps began at the Canadian factory.

Assembly of the first aircraft traditionally starts with the cockpit. On June 23, assembly of the cockpit window frame commenced at MDC's Santa Monica facility. To celebrate the occasion, Jack McGowen and John Brizendine drove the first rivet – a gold-plated sample – into the assembly.

Mock-up interior showing eight-abreast seating, center tables and a lack of centerline overhead storage compartments.

TIA's first DC-10-30CF N101TV (ln 96/msn 46800) in delivery markings.

Series 30 Launch

Because it was a buyer's market, there was a lengthy sales hiatus for both MDC and Lockheed. It was not until June 7, 1969, that the first European sales were achieved when the KSSU consortium ordered 36 DC-10-30s. The battle had been intense, with continued counteroffers from both sides. There were split opinions within the consortium, but the decision to have a common aircraft prevailed, along with the long relationship between the airlines and the Long Beach company. At the time, no breakdown of the order was made public because all four airlines still needed individual board or government approvals.

The DC-10 engine contest became as fierce as the airframe competition. Ultimately, GE CF6-50As, rated at 49,000 pounds of thrust, were selected for the KSSU aircraft, scheduled for 1973 delivery. This allowed the MTOW to increase to 530,000 pounds and the maximum payload rose to 104,000 pounds. The new range quoted was 4,750 miles with 24 first-class and 229 tourist-class passengers.

The DC-10-20 had also been offered to KSSU with the same weight and performance figures, using the JT9D-17 engine rated at 49,800 pounds thrust. Shortly after losing the campaign, P&W announced that the JT9D-17 would be withdrawn from any future offers because too many engine derivatives were being developed for what appeared to be a marginal market.

The lower deck galley complex was eliminated on the Series 30 when the consensus of the KSSU carriers decided that greater revenue could be earned by carrying belly cargo than transporting a few extra passengers. The lower cargo volume increased by 1,000 cubic feet and the belly payload jumped from 61,000 pounds to 98,500 pounds. Other differences from the Series 10 were mainly the addition of Inertial Navigation Systems (INS) and Satellite Communications (SATCOM) systems. Northwest also elected to relocate the galleys on its Series 20s to the upper deck also. However, MDC continued to offer a choice of locations on all the long-range models.

The Lockheed Approach

Lockheed had offered KSSU a new version of the TriStar, the L-1011-8.4A, with an MTOW of 575,000 pounds, powered by an RB.211-56 which would require expenditure of an additional UK£ 75 million on top of the UK£ 50 million already ready spent on development of the basic RB.211-22. This additional funding would have to be supplied by the U.K.

N101TV with revised markings, photographed in January 1979. (Author)

government and would not be easily handed over. Lockheed first needed to win an order from the ATLAS group, comprising Air France, Lufthansa, Alitalia and SABENA. It also needed a reasonable expectation of winning a number of other important orders from airlines such as British Airways, QANTAS and Singapore Airlines in the face of growing concern in the United Kingdom regarding the amount of taxpayer money being invested by the government.

The proposed L-1011-8.4A wing and tail surfaces were considerably enlarged and the fuselage stretched to add four additional seat rows. Lockheed's new offer also featured a main deck galley. Some layouts showed reduced economy-class seating so that passenger baggage could be accommodated on the main deck to increase the belly cargo volume. Deliveries were promised for spring 1973.

The DC-10 Freighter

The success of offering both DC-8 and DC-9 convertible freighter variants led MDC to provide for similar versions of the DC-10. Part of the identified potential market was military applications. At the time, the Vietnam conflict was in full swing and the U.S. Air Force's massive airlift capacity was being heavily augmented by the supplemental and scheduled airlines, particularly those with aircraft that could be operated as freighters.

However, the existence of the convertible freighter version was not made public until June 17, 1969, when Overseas National Airways (ONA) announced orders for three DC-10Fs capable of conversion to either passenger or cargo mode; an option was also taken on a fourth airplane. This order was a major milestone in the sales competition as it now restored MDC to the lead in total aircraft ordered – 183 DC-10s in four versions, versus Lockheed's 178 TriStars, all domestic models.

Again, ONA did not specify the engine type, but TIA did announce that it would adopt the same specification for its DC-10s and revise its order to two firm and two options. Deliveries to both airlines were scheduled for the spring of 1973. The contract specified a 530,000-pound MTOW that allowed the DC-10F to carry 138,500 pounds of cargo over 2,750 miles. The increased weights led to minor structural strengthening of the inner wing and some changes to the leading-edge slats.

A single-class seating arrangement allowed 330 passengers in a nine-abreast layout with a 34-inch seat-pitch to be carried 4,800 miles. Initially, the engine choice lay between the P&W JT9D-15 and a new version of the GE power plant, the CF6-50, to be rated at 47,300 pounds of thrust and available in September 1972. On July 10, ONA ordered 49,000-pound-thrust GE CF6-50A engines, and TIA followed suit on August 26.

These aircraft were officially designated as DC-10-30Fs, though MDC referred to them internally as DC-10-30CFs. The only external difference was the addition of an upward-hinging door aft of the cockpit on the left side. It was 8.5 feet high and 11.5 feet wide. The cargo handling systems were designed to fit into the existing seat tracks, the same system used on the DC-8 convertible freighters, with a lateral transfer system at the doorway. To ensure maximum passenger capacity in a long-range charter configuration, the lower galley complex was retained while the main-deck galley area and part of the elevator shafts were removable. The ceiling height restricted main-deck loads to a maximum height of 83.5 inches, mounted on twenty-three 88-inch by 125-inch pallets. To convert from cargo to passenger mode took about eight hours. There was never any intent to offer the aircraft as a Quick Change (QC) model, which had been available with the DC-9. One feature of the new version was its ability to carry a spare engine with all the ancillary equipment installed, on a special cradle that allowed the engine to be rotated to pass through the cargo doorway with ample clearance.

The KSSU Order

Swissair was the first member of KSSU to obtain board approval for an order of six firm and five options, on July 2. Interestingly, this date coincided with the disposal of its last DC-3. On August 27, KLM announced six firm plus six option orders, and UTA signed for two firm orders plus three options. SAS waited until its outgoing board chairman was replaced before making a final decision. The carrier reserved eight options but no firm orders. Lockheed's entry was rejected by KSSU because it was considered "too big and approximately $2 million more expensive" according to contemporary press reports.

At this stage, DC-10 engineering drawing releases were 95 percent complete as MDC retained its tight schedule. Wind tunnel testing reached 9,000 hours, accumulated in various tunnels. One model, 23 percent of full size, was equipped with a small jet engine to determine the airflow characteristics around the tail with the engine in reverse thrust. Other tests concentrated on fixing the location of the wing engine nacelles relative to the fuselage. The final result was the "toeing in" of the engine by two degrees. Similarly, the pitch of the nacelles was established at the most efficient cruise angle.

ONA's DC-10-30CF N1033F (ln 237/msn 46960), later destroyed in a freak accident while owned by Korean Airlines.

Swissair DC-10-30 HB-IHI (ln 241/msn 46969) in the 1977 delivery livery. Later aircraft were delivered in the colors shown on N1002X (HB-IHL, ln 292/msn 46583).

National Airlines

The next airline to announce a widebody tri-jet order was National Airlines, a Douglas customer of many years. Company president Louis B. Maytag announced on October 14 a $280-million order for nine Series 10s plus eight options. Again, it had been a tough campaign with Lockheed lasting more than one year. However, the price eventually agreed upon was the same as United's, adjusted for inflation. The initial configuration was 46 first-class and 222 coach-class; otherwise the aircraft were similar to the American Airlines specification. Deliveries were scheduled to begin in November 1971, in time for the lucrative winter route between New York and Miami. This order raised the total DC-10 sales plus options to 201.

The Pace Quickens

To accelerate DC-10 flight crew training, MDC reached an agreement in October with Flight Safety, Inc., to build an MDC-staffed flight simulator training facility adjacent to the Long Beach Air Terminal. This followed the award of a contract for the new assembly hall capable of holding six DC-10s. This location, due for completion by mid-1970, would be used to fit the vertical stabilizer, engines and final interior installations plus functional checks and customer inspections. By this time, the new engineering development center was well under construction. On November 13, the first cockpit section was delivered to Long Beach from the Santa Monica facility. There was a slight delay in delivery of the first fuselage barrels from Convair due to engineering changes, but it would have a minimal impact on the first flight date.

ATLAS Campaign

An unusual twist to the sales competition surfaced in December when Lockheed and Sud announced that talks had been held to consider naming Lockheed as the North American sales agent for the European A300B Airbus, but nothing evolved from these meetings. This arose as part of the battle between MDC and Lockheed to win the ATLAS Group, which already shared Boeing 747 maintenance programs.

Both the airframe and associated engine manufacturers faced a new hurdle. The existing DC-10-30 and the proposed long-range version of the TriStar had insufficient performance to meet Lufthansa's requirement to operate nonstop from Frankfurt to the U.S. West Coast or Rio de Janeiro with full payloads. Alitalia, then operating nonstop between Rome and Rio de Janeiro with DC-8-62s, offered a similar challenge.

MDC's solution was to increase the DC-10-30's MTOW to 555,000 pounds by extending the wingtips an additional three feet per side, expanding the total wing area to 3,610 square feet. Two additional fuel tanks were installed above and below the center wing box tank to increase the capacity by 20,000 pounds to a maximum of 240,000 pounds. Further changes included drooping the inboard ailerons and revising the flaps to improve airflow over the wing root, resulting in a 430-mile range

Named *Giuseppe Verdi,* KLM DC-10-30 PH-DTF (ln 91/msn 46555) was sold to American Airlines in 1984.

increase to 5,260 miles. To lift the increased weight, GE agreed to an up-rated CF6-50C engine rated at 51,000 pounds of thrust.

It was originally planned to airlift most of the major DC-10 components to Long Beach, particularly the fuselage barrels from San Diego and the outer wing boxes from Malton. The oversize items would be carried in the capacious Super Guppies operated by Aero Spacelines. Back-up options included shipping the San Diego-built components by barge to Long Beach harbor and trucking them to the assembly line at night. The wing boxes would be transported by rail directly to the plant, a method well established on the DC-9 program with the wings and rear fuselage sections being carried on specially modified open freight cars.

In December, a DC-10 wing mock-up was shipped to Long Beach on a suitably modified flat-bed wagon fitted with a series of strain gauges and recording devices to determine the stresses that would be placed on a wing. The experiment proved successful, so it was decided that all wings would be shipped by rail.

UTA operated DC-10s for 20 years in the colors worn by Series 30 N1341U (F-BTDB, ln 63/msn 46850).

Using aircraft as an advertising medium has become quite common in recent years.

Supporting the World Wildlife Fund, AOM's DC-10-30 F-GNDC (ln 213/msn 47849). (Roy Lock)

Advertising a seat sale in April 1991, British Airways DC-10-30 G-NIUK (ln 158/msn 46932). (Mike Axe)

Two of Canadian's DC-10-30s have been autographed; N6150Z (ln 229/msn 47889, shown) by employees and C-FCRE (ln 200/msn 47868) by VIPs and frequent fliers. (Author's Collection)

Among the first DC-10 "billboards," CP Air's Series 10 N1836U (ln 74/msn 47968) was one of two leased from United in 1983. (Author)

Canadian DC-10-30 C-GCPD (ln 281/msn 46541) was chartered by the MTV (music television) network for an around-the-world flight to record millennium events. (Exavia)

Japan Air Service DC-10-30 JA8551 (ln 437/msn 48316) operated charters to Hawaii in 1995 wearing this special "Peter Pan" scheme. (Exavia)

Rival Japan Air Charter marked one of its DC-10-40s, JA8544 (ln 340/msn 47852), for similar services in 1994. (Author's Collection)

The close relationship between Northwest and KLM is illustrated by DC-10-30 N237NW (ln 336/msn 47844) specially painted in 1999. (both Michael Bolden)

PAL DC-10-30 RP-C2114 (ln 338/msn 47838) had the honor of carrying the Pope to the Philippines in 1981. (Author's Collection)

Advertising the movie "101 Dalmatians" and its relationship with Swissair, SABENA's DC-10-30 OO-SLG (ln 170/msn 47926) is seen in March 1997. (Exavia)

To introduce its service to San Francisco in 1979, Singapore Airlines added this banner to DC-10-30 9V-SDB (ln 263/msn 46993). (Author's Collection)

Unusual recognition was made of the DC-10's last service with Swissair, on DC-10-30 HB-IHI (ln 241/msn 46969) at Zurich. (Thomas Eigenmaer)

Brazil's victory in the 1994 World Cup Soccer championship was celebrated with this specially marked DC-10-30, PP-VMD (ln 202/msn 46916). (Avimage)

AeroMexico celebrated its 50th Anniversary in 1984. Series 30 N3878P (ln 75/msn 47861) was the only DC-10 in these markings. (Author's Collection)

A Super Guppy delivers the first fuselage sections to Long Beach. The SAS DC-8-62 is LN-MOG, the 512th DC-8.

In January 1970, despite all of the improvements provided, the ATLAS group requested a delay in making a decision. At the time, the group held orders for an additional 16 Boeing 747s and over-capacity was still a problem. The airlines still could not agree on a common fleet plan. Lufthansa and SABENA preferred the TriStar while Alitalia wanted the DC-10 and Air France was still leaning towards standardizing on the Boeing 747. The group also sought lower prices than it had paid on initial Boeing 747 orders.

Lockheed's Dilemma

The price quoted to ATLAS members for the upgraded DC-10-30 was $16 million per aircraft. To be able to offer this price, MDC salesmen were renegotiating with the KSSU Group and the two supplemental airlines to get them to switch to the upgraded performance Series 30s. KSSU Group agreed in late January, and ONA and TIA accepted the changes shortly thereafter. Separate revised contracts with GE covered upgrading of the CF6-50A engines to the CF6-50C standard.

The base price for Lockheed's proposed L-1011-8.4A was estimated to be $16.6 million versus the DC-10's tag of $16 million. However, the Lockheed model's performance did not match that of the competition. For example, it was limited to 240 passengers and baggage on the Rome–Chicago route under the ground rules set by ATLAS negotiators.

To solve this problem, a second version was offered for spring 1975 delivery. Known as the L-1011-8.4D, it featured RB.211-57 power plants rated at 55,000 pounds of thrust, allowing an MTOW increase to 595,000 pounds in order to improve the payload and range. But it but would also require a new six-wheel bogie on each main landing gear. Thus, Lockheed

faced even higher development costs than MDC, by having to provide two different landing gears for the different MTOWs being contemplated. Later, Rolls-Royce somewhat alleviated this problem by promising an earlier delivery schedule for the RB.211-57 engine that eliminated the need for two different Lockheed models and gear types.

Ship One Takes Shape

The first DC-10 began to take shape in the final assembly hall on January 9, 1970, when the 55-foot-long forward fuselage barrel section arrived from San Diego aboard a Super Guppy. Within hours, it was aligned with the first cockpit section that had earlier been delivered by road from MDC's Santa Monica facility. The first wing set, shipped by rail from Canada on January 25, arrived at Long Beach on February 1. The remaining fuselage barrels arrived by air from San Diego a few days later. Meanwhile, the large aft section containing the vertical stabilizer and engine mount rapidly approached completion at Long Beach.

A major change in assembly techniques was introduced on the DC-10. Previously, most wiring and piping systems were installed after the fuselage was completed. With the DC-10's large cross-section, it was possible to install much of the systems, fitted with connectors at the manufacturing joints, at the structural subassembly phase. MDC built mini-test units that could be connected to the systems in each fuselage section for function checks before being mated with other sections.

Because the first DC-10 was considered a production aircraft and the Iron Bird had been used to take care of most installation problems ahead of time, a rapid buildup of production assemblies was achieved. To facilitate this, the number of people assigned to the DC-10 program in

MDC's Southern California facilities jumped from 10,000 in May 1969 to 14,500 by January 1970 and was to reach 20,000 by year end.

Air Afrique, headquartered at Abidjan in the Ivory Coast, made waiting for the ATLAS decision easier when, on February 23, 1970, it announced a purchase of two Series 30s plus one option, with deliveries starting in 1973. This order was not totally unexpected due to the airline's close relationship with UTA and its own fleet of DC-8s.

CF6-6 Air Test

Flight testing of the GE CF6-6 engine began on March 2, 1970 when a Boeing B-52 bomber leased from the U.S. Air Force took off at Edwards Air Force Base, California. The engine and its pod were mounted on the inboard position on the starboard wing, replacing two P&W J57 engines. The cockpit had a complete set of DC-10 engine controls and test equipment includng 900 channels of instrumentation to record test data. These tests were similar to those carried out in June 1968, when a similarly configured B-52 conducted the first air tests of the P&W JT9D engine for Boeing 747 application.

By March 30, all the fuselage sections and the wings of Ship One had been connected. On April 2, Rohr delivered the first three engine pods complete with the CF6-6 engines and all ancillary equipment already installed.

In April, MDC signed an agreement with the Yuma, Arizona Airport authorities to lease 175,000 square feet of ramp space to set up a flight-test center. The airport's desert location was ideal, with year-round good weather and minimal air traffic. Noise was not a problem since the U.S. Marine Corps had several squadrons of jet fighters based on the opposite side of the runway. At the same time, an agreement was reached with the Mexican government to allow much of the testing to be done in the almost deserted air space over Baja California that could be quickly reached via lightly used air traffic corridors. The Yuma facility would be used for most of the flight testing of all subsequent MDC jetliners and later, Boeing 717 flight trials.

DC-10 Family Proposals

Even though the DC-10 had not yet flown, MDC revealed in March that engineers were already studying three developments to the basic airframe. The first studies concentrated on a 35-foot stretch model, which could carry 348 passengers in a mixed-class layout over 4,000 miles. Another option featured a 50-foot stretch that offered a 386-passenger mixed-class capacity over 3,500 miles. Both studies kept the existing wing and were to be powered by three 51,000-pound-thrust engines while retaining the 555,000-pound MTOW.

A third proposal was a long-range version utilizing the existing fuselage, but with an extended wing. It was intended to carry 270 mixed-class passengers over 5,850 miles. Engineers also looked at combining the extended wing with the 50-foot stretch version. It was designed for a 386 mixed-class capacity over 3,700 miles. These two developments would have required power from three unspecified 54,200-pound-thrust engines.

Canadian-built wings are mated with the MDC wing box and Convair upper fuselage.

The DC-10 Twin Emerges Again

Another study produced the twin-engine model, still identified as the D-969C. Officially called "236-seat Twin (DC-10 derivative)," it was more popularly known as the DC-10 Twin. The design requirement remained to carry 236 mixed-class passengers over a 1,540-mile range. A number of alternatives were examined. For example, the D-969C-4 showed the DC-10 forward fuselage section reduced by 200 inches. The wing embodied the Series 30 6-foot wingspan extension to improve short-field performance. Another study, the D-969C-6 was issued at about the same time using the same fuselage, but reduced the wingspan by four feet and increased the vertical stabilizer height by a foot.

In both cases, the DC-10 horizontal stabilizer and landing gear was utilized. The DC-10 Twin retained the 51,000-pound-thrust engines based

A view of the Building 84 production line. Due to ceiling height, the vertical stabilizers were added on the ramp.

The GE CF-6 engine was initially air-tested on a Boeing B-52A leased from the U.S. Air Force.

on an MTOW of 316,000 pounds. Other design parameters included a Maximum Landing Weight (MLW) of 284,000 pounds, Zero Fuel Weight (ZFW) of 265,000 pounds and Operator's Empty Weight (OEW) of 201,270 pounds. Some sources suggest that this would have been re-designated DC-11 if produced. However, management rejected using this designation because of concern that it might be dubbed DC-10-11, too close to the competitor's designation. Several other fuselage lengths were also studied with mixed-class seating between 197 and 308 passengers.

Paper Freighters

A spin-off from the DC-10 Twin was an all-cargo version called the DC-10-C-2, designed to carry a 100,000-pound payload over a 1,200-mile range. It would have featured a high wing and swing nose for cargo loading. A less radical design, the DC-10-C-4, would have utilized the basic DC-10 structure with an MTOW of 540,000 pounds to carry 200,000 pounds of cargo over a 2,800-mile range. Four pylon-mounted engines

were to be carried under the low wing. Tradeoff studies were also done utilizing greater thrust engines in both this version and a stretched model that would have weighed 650,000 pounds at takeoff.

Perhaps the ultimate study was the DC-10-C-6, a 1.4-million-pound MTOW aircraft capable of carrying 400,000-pound loads over a 4,200-mile range. The low wing had a span of 255 feet and overall length of 248 feet. Initially, power was to come from six 60,000-pound-thrust engines, but later studies reflected four 70,000-pound-thrust power plants. A 1.1 million-pound MTOW variant of this design differed in that it would carry the same payload over a 3,000-mile range, retaining the same basic dimensions as its bigger companion.

More Power to Pratt & Whitney

In mid-May 1970, Northwest Airlines agreed to an amended contract with MDC and P&W to improve the performance of its DC-10-20s. The JT9D-15 takeoff thrust would increase from 45,500 pounds of thrust to 47,000 pounds with the assistance of water injection. The additional power allowed a 10,000-pound increase in the MTOW, to 525,000 pounds, and extended the range to 4,065 miles. The engine manufacturer also announced that work was progressing to introduce an advanced version with 50,000 pounds thrust using water injection. This would allow the Series 20's MTOW to grow to 548,000 pounds and increase the payload range to 4,460 miles with a full load of 255 passengers (mixed-class) and baggage.

Flight Test Plan

Details of the flight-test schedule were also released in May, with a total of 1,500 hours of flight testing scheduled with five aircraft flying an average of 33 hours each per month. To maintain the tight schedule, data reduction was accelerated by heavy application of computers and in-flight transmission of data via telemetry to ground stations, in order to give real-time information while the test was in progress. Four hundred channels of data could be transmitted simultaneously at ranges of up to 250 miles from the ground receiver. The introduction of telemetry for flight-test data recording would help increase the aircraft utilization by reducing down time; the DC-8 test fleet had averaged 27 hours per aircraft per month.

The DC-10 Twin was the subject of many sales discussions with airlines in 1970.

The DC-10 cockpit and flight engineer's panel. These particular layouts were featured on ATLAS aircraft.

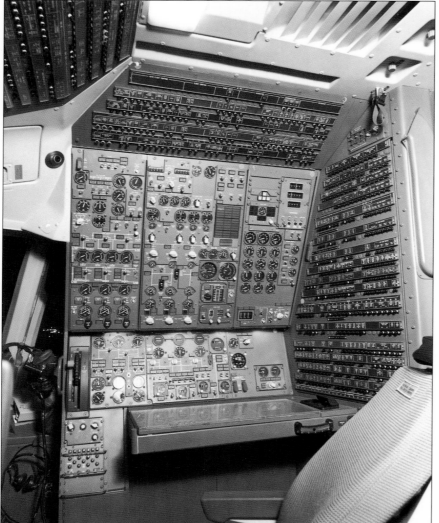

Each aircraft would be tasked with a primary test program plus a secondary assignment to increase utilization and provide backup. The first flight was scheduled for September 15 with Ship One (436 test hours planned) designated as the primary stability and control aircraft. Ship Three (373 hours) was allotted performance testing and would be the second to fly. This was because Ship Two (287 hours) was allocated for ground-based static load testing prior to flying. It would handle flight guidance and control tests plus demonstration flights. Ship Four (254 hours) was slated for systems testing while the fifth (150 hours) would operate function and reliability flights.

Static Testing

One June 12, Ship Two, which would be subjected to static proof loading, was delivered to the new Engineering Test Facility, the first time a complete aircraft of this size was to be used for this test. Douglas had developed a technique whereby the entire aircraft was supported by computer-controlled jacks that allowed programmed loads to be applied differentially. Only the landing gear was tied down to jacks anchored on the floor. This approach was inaugurated earlier by Douglas engineers while working on a service-life extension program on the Douglas C-124 Globemaster military transport.

The overall test cost was reduced by 25 percent as it did away with the need for a large steel supporting structure. And, since the need to reset the manual jacks and relocate sand bags under the old scheme was gone, time to completion was reduced by 50 percent. Testing began on July 15 and was completed before Ship One made its maiden flight. The loads applied exceeded 1.5 times those expected in service. After completing the trials, Ship Two was returned to the production line for completion. All the strain gauges and recording devices were left in place because Ship Two would be used for air loads measurement in addition to the other tasks scheduled during the flight-test program.

Alitalia Breaks Ranks

On June 15, Alitalia announced that, subject to board approval, it was ordering four GE CF6-50A-powered DC-10-30s for $17 million each with options for a further eight. Deliveries were to commence in 1973. This brought the order book to 103 firm and 111 options. This decision, no doubt, was made in part due to the amount of offset work that MDC had contracted to Italian factories, but the long traditional relationship was also a key factor.

The doors of the new Fit and Functions building frame Ship One at the rollout ceremony.

The official rollout of the first DC-10 took place on July 23, 1970, just 50 years and one day since the founding of the Douglas Aircraft Company. The ceremony took place at the new hangar in front of more than 1,000 invited onlookers. Heading the guest list was Spiro T. Agnew, vice president of the United States, California Governor Ronald Reagan and a host of Congressmen including the Chairman of the House Armed Services Committee, Senator Mendel Rivers.

To formally initiate the rollout, Agnew, James McDonnell and Donald Douglas Sr. jointly pushed three throttles open on a mounted control quadrant. It started an unusual presentation because the guests were seated in the hangar while the gleaming DC-10 slowly taxied past under its own power, having been parked out of sight at the side of the building. Leading the aircraft were 50 Scottish bagpipers in full regalia, reflecting the heritage of both McDonnell and Douglas. When the aircraft stopped, boarding stairs were positioned and representative flight attendants from the 12 customer airlines disembarked to form a guard of honor as the VIPs boarded the aircraft. The interior was complete except for the installation of seats and galleys. Even the carpeting had been installed. Some of the space was already filled with flight-test data recorders, mounted on the seat tracks.

Four more DC-10s were already structurally complete at the time of the rollout. The DC-10's debut beat the TriStar by just over a month, in spite of the later program launch. The first TriStar rolled out at Lockheed's new Palmdale facility on September 1.

Additional Orders

A week after rollout, during the 1970 Paris Air Show, MDC announced that UTA had exercised two of the three previously placed options for DC-10-30s on July 30. Later the same day, Continental Airlines announced an order for eight DC-10-10s plus options for a further eight. As the Air Show progressed, the New Zealand government also approved Air New

Aboard Ship One at the ceremony, Old Mac's audience includes (left to right): California Governor Ronald Reagan, Donald Douglas Jr., Donald Douglas Sr. and Vice President Spiro T. Agnew.

Zealand's purchase of three Series 30s plus one option. Finnair signed for two Series 30 options as part of a package that included eight used DC-9 Series 10s, but the deal was not firmed up until January 1971.

Spurred by Alitalia's decision, Lufthansa protected five delivery slots with a Letter of Intent (LOI) signed on August 6. The contract was signed on September 23 for four Series 30s. On August 7, SABENA signed an LOI for two Series 30s. Both SABENA and Lufthansa also purchased undisclosed numbers of options. Air Afrique amended its previous order to three firm plus two options on the same day, bringing the total announced orders and options to 241 from 15 airlines.

A partial cause of this flurry was an announcement that MDC was about to raise prices by four percent to cover inflation and was offering attractive trade-in terms. But the most important reason was Lockheed's failure to announce the launch of a long-range version of the TriStar. Air New Zealand in particular had been under strong political pressure to buy the type, but Lockheed needed orders for at least 30 to 50 aircraft before committing to production. TWA and Air Canada had agreements to convert options to the new model, but TWA only needed eight and Air Canada required four. British Airways, the major potential customer, was considering standardizing on the Boeing 747 and not ready to make a move. Air France, facing possible simultaneous introduction of the Concorde, A-300 and Mercure at the time either tri-jet would be entering service, also preferred staying with the Boeing 747 as its primary option.

During this hectic period, Lockheed gained one customer, PSA, with an order for five TriStars, though only two would ever be delivered as the aircraft proved too big for the Los Angeles–San Francisco route for which it was originally intended. TriStar sales then totaled 178; Air Jamaica had placed an order for two aircraft in April.

Money Matters

Japan Air Lines (JAL) became the target of a brief competition between MDC and Boeing in early August. JAL, already in negotiation with Boeing for the high-density Boeing 747SR for domestic services, invited MDC officials to enter a bid for a stretched DC-10 capable of carrying the same number of passengers. Lewis and McGowen went to Tokyo in mid-August to discuss the possibilities. Their major concerns were meeting a 1975 delivery requirement and the additional development costs of introducing yet another new model so soon.

MDC was approaching its maximum requirement for cash flow as DC-10 production gathered pace. In July, the corporation had withdrawn a public offering for $100 million in four-year notes when stock market conditions became unattractive. In conjunction with this offering, MDC arranged a bank credit of $400 million and was negotiating to increase its credit line to $500 million.

To date, approximately $800 million had been spent on the DC-10 program, all raised from DC-8/DC-9 earnings and military sales, plus progress payments on existing DC-10 orders. The need for additional cash arose from several causes including declining returns as the backlog for first-generation jet airliners decreased. The unanticipated costs of developing the Series 30CF and earlier than planned higher-gross-weight versions of the Series 30 were also to be reckoned with. In addition, low introductory prices contributed to the dilemma. As a result, the break-even point had moved steadily beyond the original 200 aircraft figure predicted in May 1968. After considering all these points, MDC declined to offer a stretched DC-10 to JAL.

First Flight

Some 20,000 employees and families gathered on Saturday, August 29, 1970, at 10 a.m. to watch the first DC-10 take to the air, two weeks ahead of the previous target date of September 15. Lightly loaded at 340,000 pounds, it was airborne in just under 5,000 feet. Earlier, the aircraft

completed some taxi trials and low-speed runs down the main Long Beach Airport runway.

DC-10 Project pilot Cliff Stout was at the controls, assisted by Harris Van Valkenburg. John Chamberlain was the flight engineer and Shojun Yukawa monitored the test data readouts. The tri-jet was carrying 25,000 pounds of instrumentation to support 2,300 sensors that recorded 360 million data points per hour. This information was transferred by telemetry to antennae atop 8,400-foot-high Frost Peak in the San Gabriel Mountains, then via a ground data link to Long Beach.

Three hours and 26 minutes after departure, Ship One landed at Edwards Air Force Base, after reaching an altitude of 30,000 feet and cruising at 300 knots. During the flight, the crew had checked out basic handling characteristics, various systems and completed a functional test of the data recording and transmission systems. Flutter tests went so well that they were terminated 30 minutes ahead of schedule. Feeling comfortable with the aircraft, the pilots performed a chandelle maneuver shortly before landing. Stout was impressed with the performance, and the crew reported that it flew "like a swan," with no squawks to report. Just 28 months had elapsed since Old Mac had given the go ahead. By now, final assembly of the tenth DC-10 had begun.

Testing Continues

A second flight lasting one hour and 40 minutes was flown two days later during which full stalls were undertaken with the landing gear up and gear down. The crew complement increased to six with chief test pilot Heimie Heimerdinger and flight engineer John Cook added to the list. Within a week, eight flights had accumulated 18 hours and 55 minutes flying time. The aircraft then returned to Long Beach for continued testing.

By the end of September, more than 52 hours had been accumulated during 23 flights. The tests were progressing so well that MDC speculated that the program would be reduced to 1,250 hours of flight testing with certification date by August 1971. The flutter envelope had been cleared to Mach 0.89 at 35,000 feet, and the aircraft had flown at an MTOW of 352,000 pounds. Flutter was induced by the addition of small vanes on the extremities of the wing and tail surfaces and damped out very quickly of its own accord. Airborne engine restarts were accomplished at a speed of 300 knots at 10,000 feet.

Ship One had logged more than 100 hours by October 6 and had demonstrated takeoffs with one engine out by shutting down either the center or one of the wing-mounted power plants. The stall speed program was completed and much of the control testing at extreme Centers of Gravity (CG) was well underway. Several flights exceeding five hours had been trouble-free and the GE CF-6 engines' fuel consumption was showing better than the guaranteed figures.

Resplendent in American Airlines livery, Ship Three made a flight of three hours and 15 minutes on October 26. After a landing at Yuma, it returned to Long Beach. By then, Ship One had completed 85 hours of test flying.

Lockheed's Problems

The Lockheed TriStar made its maiden flight from Palmdale on November 16. About this time, Lockheed began to run into serious financial problems stemming from the C-5A program and its large cost overruns, forcing the company to seek an urgent settlement with the U.S. Government. The outcome of this was critical to the TriStar cash requirements. Rolls-Royce was also facing a similar situation. The high cost of developing the RB.211 using new technology and trying to hold costs down to match GE's prices began to create problems.

End of a Great Year

A proposed integration of American and Western Airlines was announced on November 2, which would strongly influence Western in its

Ship One (msn 46500) lifts off on its August 29, 1970 maiden flight. (Author)

choice of widebody tri-jets later the following year. The merger faced a long, drawn-out battle when Continental and others strongly objected to the CAB.

Airkapital, a German financial group, purchased two Series 30s on November 18, on behalf of Frankfurt-based Atlantis Airways, for deliveries in April and December 1973. Atlantis already operated DC-8s and DC-9-32s in Inclusive Tour Charter (ITC) services, but unfortunately this order was subsequently canceled when Atlantis went into bankruptcy in October 1972.

At the end of November, SABENA announced that the two Series 30s it had ordered in August would be DC-10-30CFs. The airline had selected the convertible version at the time of signing the LOI, but chose to delay the announcement for internal reasons.

The exciting year of 1970 closed out for MDC on December 23 when Ship Four, in United markings, made a first flight lasting five hours and 10 minutes. This raised the cumulative DC-10 flight time to 235 hours during 119 flights. The flight envelope had then expanded to include Mach 0.95 dive speeds from 35,000 feet and a peak altitude of 42,000 feet.

Series 20 Improvements

In early January 1971, MDC announced that the Series 20 would match the Series 30's 555,000-pound MTOW for 1973 deliveries. To achieve this, Pratt & Whitney had promised that the JT9D-25W, generating 50,000 pounds of takeoff thrust, would be available. The "W" signified water injection, to be used to create the extra power. Test bed results showed that water injection worked very well and did not produce the smoky exhaust trails associated with the older models that had become known as "water wagons."

Rolls-Royce Insolvency

Rolls-Royce admitted that it was insolvent on January 22, 1971, and sought protection under the bankruptcy provisions just four days later. The timing could not have been worse for the company. In a recent election, the Conservatives who intended to withdraw state aid for private firms had ousted the U.K. Labor government that had long bankrolled ailing private companies to save jobs. Naturally, this sent shock waves through Lockheed management, which was still battling its own financial problems. Lockheed had a $400 million credit line with a syndicate of 24 banks. The company claimed that it was owed $750 million by the U.S. Government, but had to settle for just $480 million at the end of January,

The first-flight crew (left to right): Clifford L. Stout, DC-10 project pilot; Harris C. Van Valkenburg, deputy chief test pilot; John D. Chamberlain, flight engineer; and Shojun Yukawa, flight-test engineer.

so cash remained in short supply. Rolls-Royce was officially placed in the hands of a receiver on February 4. The British Government then announced that it would take over all of the military engine programs in the national interest, but would not support the R.B.211 project.

Because the situation looked grim for the L-1011, MDC salesmen began offering DC-10s with some fairly strong incentives for TriStar customers to switch. Eventually, reports of this activity reached the attention of the Senate Banking Committee through Senator William Proxmire. This salesmanship was considered illegal under the Clayton Act, which says in effect, "You can't lure a customer away if he already has a signed contract in place with someone else." Because Lockheed had yet to say it couldn't produce the aircraft, MDC was told to cease and desist. In hindsight, whether the tactic would have worked is doubtful, because agreements already in place with existing DC-10 customers required MDC to give retroactive price cuts to match any offers made to new buyers

Fluctuating Orders

Meanwhile, the financial recession that was still rampaging in the United States led United managers to announce, on January 27, that the

SABENA was the only scheduled airline to specify DC-10-30CFs for its fleet. OO-SLE (ln 330/msn 47836) appears in original colors. Changes introduced in 1984 are shown below on OO-SLA (ln 115/msn 47906). Bottom, OO-SLH (ln 190/msn 47927), leased from Lufthansa in 1994, wears the current markings.

Mark Busseniers

Exavia

The original N101AA (In 2/msn 46501) appears at Yuma in January 1971. Note the "Astroliner" titles on the nose. (Gerry Markgraf)

airline was canceling eight firm DC-10 orders and dropping 15 options. However, the good news on that same day was that the FAA issued the DC-10 type inspection authorization signaling the start of the official flight demonstration phase leading to certification. Ship Two joined the flight-test fleet on January 29. A few days later, night flying was initiated at Yuma to accelerate the program.

By mid-March, 550 hours of testing had been completed during 300 flights. Reliability was so good that as many as 10 flights a day were being flown by the four aircraft. Two of the DC-10s were fitted with pre-production CF-6s, while the other pair had production engines installed. The latter were now rated at 40,000 pounds of thrust. As a standard part of the tests, takeoffs had been completed at 10,000 pounds over the specified MTOW, with landings at 380,000 pounds, or 32,000 pounds above the design limit.

Good News and Bad News

National exercised two options in February for two Series 30s to be used on its Miami–London route but dropped the remaining six options. Because of its concern over the Lockheed situation, Delta took the precaution of quietly signing an LOI for five DC-10-10s on March 21. However, to ease its cash flow in view of a firm contract with Lockheed,

Delta immediately sold the DC-10s to United and leased them back for a minimum period of 30 months. An Export-Import Bank announcement issued in May stated that approval had been given for loans to Lufthansa to finance seven DC-10s, not four as previously publicly announced by the airline.

In a routine filing with the Stock Exchange Commission in early May, MDC revealed that, in addition to United's canceled buys, American had dropped 10 options on April 30. MDC also stated that it had already invested $1.215 billion in the DC-10 program and would probably need an additional $400 million by the end of 1971. To offset this, the company showed a firm DC-10 backlog worth $1.972 billion. Overall, MDC still retained a backlog of $2.1 billion.

Provisional Type Certificate

The FAA issued a provisional type certificate for the DC-10 on May 24, which meant that FAA inspectors could issue individual airworthiness certificates for each aircraft. This permitted MDC to deliver DC-10s to customers for crew training and simulated services over their route systems.

The first aircraft to receive this document was Ship Eight which, still in house colors, flew to the 1971 Paris Air Show on May 31, via St. Louis. For the flight, the DC-10 was named *Spirit of St. Louis*. At the air show, MDC

DC-10-10 N60NA (In 14/msn 46700) *Barbara*, renamed *Suzanne* in 1975.

A major sales coup was selling DC-10s to Lufthansa. Top, Series 30 D-ADHO (ln 190/msn 47927) appears on a pre-delivery test flight. Above, the markings were revised in 1989; D-ADFO (ln 166/msn 47925) was withdrawn in 1994 and converted to a freighter for Gemini Air Cargo.

announced that initial DC-10 deliveries would be made to American and United at a joint ceremony on June 29. A similar ceremony had been held at the Douglas Aircraft Santa Monica factory when the first DC-6s were delivered to both airlines simultaneously on November 24, 1946.

Lockheed Salvation

After many high-level talks between British and American government officials and Lockheed management, the U.K. Government agreed to provide financial assistance to Rolls-Royce, subject to a substantial increase in price of the engines. It was to cost the airlines an additional $640,000 for each TriStar, most of it payable in advance. Lockheed's banks also agreed to lend a further $250 million for the TriStar program provided that the U.S. Government would guarantee the loan.

On May 6, Treasury Secretary John Connelly formally asked Congress to approve a federal loan guarantee. It was to squeak through Congress on August 2 by just one vote.

One of the few remaining DC-10 certification tasks was completed on July 2 with the successful evacuation in just 86 seconds of 345 passengers and a crew of 10 from a DC-10 in a darkened hangar. The test was monitored by the FAA and watched by representatives of the customer airlines and members of the Air Line Pilots Association.

By mid-July, the DC-10 flight-test program had exceeded 1,500 hours; only the auto-land testing was incomplete. Ship Two had made the first automatic landing on March 27 under the command of Cliff Stout who was responsible for most of the auto-land testing. More than 100 automatic landings had been completed by July 8, when the FAA was shown that the aircraft could operate to Category II Instrument Landing System (ILS) approaches, down to 1,200-foot forward runway visibility at a 100-foot decision height. Although Category II certification was originally scheduled for the same October date targeted for full FAA certification of the aircraft, it would be approved in early August. With the flight-test program progressing so smoothly, the FAA certification date was moved ahead by almost three months.

Ship One at Edwards Air Force Base during a "VMu" MTOW takeoff test, at full aft-center of gravity with no flaps and the rear fuselage touching the ground.

DC-10-10 N1801U (ln 4/msn 46600) climbs out at Long Beach with asymmetrical slats, during an August 1971 test flight. The red paint was applied for ice buildup observation. (Author)

Named *Spirit of St. Louis,* Ship Eight (N1803U, msn 46602) poses at the MDC St. Louis facility with a replica of its namesake. Ship Eight was en route to the 1971 Paris Air Show.

Chapter VIII
INTO SERVICE

Old Mac hands over the keys to the first two DC-10s, delivered to American and United.

The DC-10 Type and Production Certificates were issued by FAA Administrator John H. Schaffer on July 29, 1971, just 11 months after the first flight. The flight-test program had logged 1,551 hours during 929 flights. The DC-10 was the first commercial transport to be certified under new Federal Air Regulation (FAR) Part 36 noise guidelines. Following certification, Old Mac handed over the symbolic golden keys of the first two DC-10s to Marion Saddler, vice chairman of American Airlines and Edward Carlson, president of United.

American Airlines staged a public relations coup when a number of VIPs, including former Chairman C. R. Smith, Donald Douglas Sr. and 1930s film actress Gloria Swanson, arrived in a DC-3 wearing an original American Airlines livery. During the ceremonies, another DC-3 was positioned next to the two DC-10s, with seven more tri-jets lining the flight ramp.

After the ceremonies, the two DC-10s taxied out for takeoff. American left first. During United's takeoff run, the pilot aborted before rotation and returned to the end of the runway. The co-pilot's sliding window had not been latched properly and slid open during acceleration. After locking it, the United DC-10 rapidly departed.

During the press conference, Old Mac stunned everyone by admitting, in response to a question from a reporter, that the DC-10 break-even number was now 438 aircraft, plus or minus five percent. Break-even numbers are almost never publicly revealed. Mr. McDonnell also stated that the company had spent $1.5 billion of private capital on the DC-10 development. Considering the Lockheed loan situation – under heated debate in Congress at the time – the comments were quite remarkable and obviously intended for political ears. At the same conference, CAB Chairman Secor Brown also speculated that the next big engine development would have to come from the French since there was no government support for U.S. manufacturers.

First Service

Because of the low load factors still being experienced by the domestic airlines, American and United removed a number of seats and installed lounges in both the first-class and coach sections of the newly acquired DC-10s. These changes were made by the airlines at their own facilities immediately after delivery. American reduced seating capacity to 206 and positioned its first-class lounge at the front of the aircraft and the coach lounge at the rear. United placed both lounges adjacent to the upper galley complex, reducing seating to 222. With the addition of the lounges, American changed its planned "DC-10 Astroliner" designation to "DC-10 LuxuryLiner." However, Ships Two and Three did wear the Astroliner titles during the flight-testing period.

A race began between American and United to be the first into service with the DC-10. American initially stated it would inaugurate services between Chicago and Washington, D.C., then switched to Chicago–Los Angeles on August 17. United had planned to start on the same route on September 15, but settled for August 14 on the San Francisco–Washington route. American finally launched a 9:45 a.m. DC-10 departure (Flight 184) from Los Angeles to Chicago on August 5, simply because all preparations were complete and no further training required. American's rush to get the first DC-10 into service also allowed it to free up a Boeing 747 from the Los Angeles–Chicago route re-assigning it to the New York–San Juan route which would soon enter its peak season.

Apart from a number of senior MDC guests, two other Long Beach employees were aboard the American inaugural. Henry Oborski, a quality control inspector, had been aboard every scheduled first flight of a Douglas aircraft since the DC-4. Shop worker Don Dodge Jr. and his wife Cecyl were the first to reserve seats for the inaugural DC-10 flight in scheduled service no matter when or where it might take place.

American Airlines DC-10-10 N102AA (ln 3/msn 46502) on short finals at Los Angeles, wearing the early "DC-10 LuxuryLiner" titles. (Author)

Another Setback

The U.S. Congress added another setback to both MDC and Lockheed in mid-August. To be more competitive in the international markets, the decision had been made to take the U.S. dollar off the gold standard and force a currency revaluation. Part of this change included the introduction of a 10-percent surcharge on all imported goods.

For the DC-10, its incoming wings from Canada plus fuselage panels and associated components from Italy increased the cost by approximately $300,000 per aircraft. A similar cost was incurred for the L-1011's imported engines. In spite of Lockheed's ongoing struggle to survive, the Treasury refused to provide a waiver. Naturally, these costs were passed on to the domestic customers. Foreign airlines were exempt since the items were being re-exported after aircraft delivery.

On the bright side, MDC signed a contract with Aeronaves de Mexico for two Series 30s in August, the first to be sold south of the border.

Production Line Speeds Up

The first two DC-10s in service had accumulated more than 800 flight hours when American Airlines' second aircraft was delivered, on September 20. On the production line, the first Series 20 for Northwest (Ship No. 28) was structurally complete and assembly of the 41st aircraft had already begun. Company test pilots had completed 365 automatic landings.

SAS, still concerned over the industry's over-capacity problems, finally confirmed the purchase of two Series 30s and continued its remaining six options after board approval on September 29. On the same day, Western ordered four Series 10s that were part of American's options, based on the assumption that the CAB would not approve the merger mentioned earlier. However, if it did go through, the aircraft would remain part of the American order. Interestingly, American made the progress payments pending the CAB's decision. Western also indicated that, should the merger be denied, it would buy a total of nine DC-10-10s. This brought the overall order book to 133 firm and 90 options from 20 airlines. The CAB subsequently denied the merger.

The Western order was the first to stipulate a 30,000-pound increase in MTOW, to 440,000 pounds. The augmentation allowed an optional 32,700-pound auxiliary fuel tank below the center section to be activated, giving the aircraft ample reserves for the Minneapolis-to-Honolulu route. The increase in MTOW also required a slightly thicker lower wing skin to be installed. Eventually, all Series 10s were brought up to this standard. An interim MTOW of 430,000 pounds was also available, but none of airlines selected this option.

Meanwhile, National Airlines became the third DC-10 operator with the delivery of its first aircraft on October 22, 1971.

Battle for Japan

With the European sales campaign nearly over, the Japanese market became the scene of a bitterly fought sales contest, which eventually resulted in the ousting of Japan's Prime Minister. All three American manufacturers formed alliances with Japanese trading companies to gain an advantage in negotiating with the two major airlines, Japan Air Lines (JAL) and All Nippon Airways (ANA). MDC elected to join forces with Mitsui and Company. The stakes were large, with the carriers thought to require as many as 25 aircraft each.

In mid-1971, Mitsui, which had shares in ANA, believed that the DC-10-10 would be chosen by ANA and arranged an unannounced purchase of six Series 10s on behalf of ANA to ensure early availability. Unbeknown to Mitsui, ANA management had already opted for the TriStar in March.

Japan Air Lines required additional Boeing 747s and a small number of long-range tri-jets. However, JAL managers were not in a rush to buy the second type as the company was still taking delivery of DC-8-62s and Boeing 747s for overseas routes. Lockheed's strategy was to win ANA at all costs since it appeared to be the largest order.

To prevent ANA from taking the DC-10s from Mitsui, Lockheed president Carl Kotchian set up means of making payoffs to Japanese Prime Minister Tanaka, his political party and key ANA managers. Kotchian's plan was to let MDC and Boeing win the JAL orders so that the ANA deal would be less likely to attract attention. At one point, he was shocked to learn that JAL was leaning towards the TriStar. A win here would have been embarrassing as the long-range TriStar had yet to be launched and a commitment to build it was not in sight.

The Payoffs Succeed

Kotchian's efforts bore fruit when ANA announced in November that it had selected the TriStar and placed an order for six, though the formal contract was not signed until October 1972. This news stunned Mitsui, as the company was not geared to re-market the DC-10s. Several of the aircraft were in the subassembly process, so Mitsui enlisted the help of MDC to sell the aircraft on its behalf. MDC salesmen worked hard to find near-term operators, but none of the major world airlines were in a position to absorb any additional widebody jets on short notice. This led to expanding the search to the smaller operators.

AeroMexico's DC-10-30s were delivered in the bare metal scheme seen above on XA-DUG (In 147/msn 46936). Below, DC-10-30 XA-RIY (In 75/msn 47861) in 1994 wears a new livery created after AeroMexico was privatized.

Delivered in 1973, Western DC-10-10 N901WA (In 95/msn 46908) was sold as N166AA to American Airlines. Just prior to its demise, Western adopted a bare metal scheme shown below on a Series 10 departing from San Francisco.

Aftermath

During Tanaka's bribery scandal trial and the 1974 U.S. Senate Subcommittee hearings chaired by Senator Frank Church, it was revealed that Lockheed's payoffs to Japanese officials had totaled $12 million. This information only emerged by accident when the Church committee was investigating Northrop payments to President Nixon's campaign fund. Senior Northrop executive Tom Jones testified that Northrop only did what Lockheed had been doing for many years to win foreign military contracts. The Securities & Exchange Commission (SEC) had already started looking into all the manufacturers' overseas business dealings. Just prior to the start of the Church committee hearings on Lockheed's dealings, a Lockheed press statement admitted that a total of $22 million had been paid out between 1970 and 1975 during worldwide negotiations.

Wearing the traditional Viking long boat cheatline, SAS DC-10-30 SE-DFD (ln 174/msn 46869) was sold to AOM after several years on lease.

A Speed Record

National's third DC-10 established a speed record during its Long Beach-to-Miami delivery flight on December 22. It covered the 2,326-mile trip in three hours, 38 minutes and 42 seconds, bettering the old DC-8 record by more than 20 minutes. Just a week earlier, National had begun scheduled DC-10 service between New York and Miami. At the time, the airline adorned its aircraft with women's names in connection with a controversial sales campaign. In an era that included mini-skirt uniforms, a smiling female flight attendant introduced herself and added, "Fly me." The female names were later dropped.

National had the distinction of introducing a new type of evacuation slide which also did double duty as a life raft without any modifications. The DC-10 carried four 60-seat and four 25-seat rafts, which replaced the old cumbersome models previously carried by overwater airliners. The advantage of the new slide raft was that the simple act of pulling the release deployed the unit for either application.

United rounded the year off nicely for MDC on December 22 by announcing that it had firmed up three options for 1974-75 delivery and was retaining its seven remaining options.

Operational Problems

Though the flight deck crews were enamored with the DC-10's performance – particularly with the engines – a few small problems were emerging for the flight attendants. As a fuel savings effort, crews were flying the aircraft at cruise speeds of Mach 0.82 instead of Mach 0.85 at 35,000 feet. This saved about 1,000 pounds of fuel per flight hour, but caused the aircraft to cruise with a three-degree nose-up attitude, making it difficult for the flight attendants to push the heavier carts "uphill," towards the nose.

As with any new type entering service, the usual minor bugs – particularly with avionics – were encountered, but only two flight cancellations occurred during the first five months. Both American and United were very careful with the DC-10 scheduling. Under an agreement in place due to the excess capacity situation, the addition of a DC-10 on a route resulted in two narrowbody services being withdrawn from the same city pair.

DC-10-30 I-DYNE (ln 88/msn 47862) served with Alitalia for 10 years before being traded to MDC which leased it to AeroMexico.

Shortly after entering service, some United Series 10s were adorned with the "DC-10 Friendship" titles as shown on N1817U (ln 86/msn 46616) at Yuma in 1973. Deliveries in 1974 had the small titles as seen below on Series 10 N1841U (ln 298/msn 46634).

United experimented briefly with a bare-metal finish below the cheatline, as evidenced on DC-10-10 N1811U (ln 32/msn 46610). (Thomas Livesey)

Air Afrique replaced its DC-8s with DC-10-30s including TU-TAN (ln 288/msn 46997), which was sold to AOM in 1995.

DC-10-30 ZK-NZM (ln 116/msn 47847), one of eight operated by Air New Zealand.

Firm Orders and Options – December 1971

	Series-10		Series-20		Series-30		
	Firm	Option	Firm	Option	Firm	Option	
Aeronaves de Mexico					2	0	
Air Afrique					3	2	
Air New Zealand					3	1	
Alitalia					4	6	
American	25	11					
Atlantis					2	0	
Continental	8	8					
Delta	5	3					
Finnair					2	2	
KLM					6	6	
Lufthansa					4	0	
National	9	0			2	0	
Northwest			14	14			
Overseas National *					3	3	
SABENA *					2	0	
SAS					2	6	
Swissair					5	5	
Trans International *					2	2	
United	25	7					
UTA					4	4	
Western	4	0					
TOTAL	**76**	**29**	**14**	**14**	**46**	**37**	**= 216**

* Series 30F

Meeting a Decision Maker

In the early 1970s, this author was a market research analyst at MDC working for R.E.G. Davies, a well-known airline historian. My assigned task was to specialize in non-scheduled airlines, particularly those based in Europe.

When the Mitsui-All Nippon deal fell through, the MDC sales staff was asked to assist in finding new homes for the aircraft, some of which were already in final assembly. Efforts to sell them to major carriers had met with little success due to the excess capacity situation at the time.

In November 1971, Freddie Laker had a small fleet of Boeing 707s and BAC 1-11s. He was having trouble with U.K. authorities regarding some of the 707 affinity charters he was operating across the North Atlantic. As a result, Laker began publicizing his concept of a low-cost, no-frills scheduled service named "Skytrain." With his reputation as an entrepreneur and innovator, it struck me that Laker might jump at the chance to become the first DC-10 operator in Europe. I mentioned my idea to sales director Don Talmage who was responsible for non-scheduled airlines, and he asked me to go to London for a talk with Laker himself. U.K.-based salesman Jackson Kelly was assigned to accompany me.

After a short briefing on the DC-10's capability, early availability, and pricing, Laker opened his office door and called down the hall for his sales, maintenance and financial directors to come and listen to my informal presentation. A short session of questions followed, then Freddie asked each director in turn if they thought they could handle it if he acquired two aircraft. The maintenance director thought it was possible provided they could get assistance with heavy checks from a carrier like American Airlines. The salesman thought he could fill the seats because even lower fares could be offered. The finance director said he would need help to raise the financing, but we pointed out that Mitsui would be willing to help.

Freddie then chatted about the Skytrain project for a while and suddenly said that he would take two DC-10s provided we would provide support, particularly with arranging the financing.

When we phoned Long Beach to tell them, there was disbelief that so much had been achieved during such a short visit. A further series of visits by MDC and Mitsui personnel finally put the package together.

The final meeting took place in January 1972, in a suite at London's Dorchester Hotel. The lead negotiator for MDC was vice president of marketing Charles Forsyth, a charismatic man of generous proportions and aptly known in-house as "the wide-bodied salesman." Laker and Forsyth closeted themselves in a room while others were working outside on various details. When the two emerged a few hours later, Forsyth was shirtless. To the startled onlookers, he announced that, "We struck a deal, but Freddie took the shirt off my back!"

One of the world's oldest charter airlines, Martinair has operated many Douglas types, including DC-10-30CF PH-MBG (ln 127/msn 46891).

A Good Start to 1972

The year 1972 started well with orders from TIA, which converted one of its options to a firm buy on January 13 and Iberia, which ordered three firm and five options for Series 30s on January 17. Laker Airways surprised everyone with an order for two Series 10s on February 23. Laker's aircraft would be the first configured in a 345-passenger layout. Two days later, Dutch charter airline Martinair became the 23rd customer with an order for a single Series 30F convertible model. At Martinair's request, MDC designed a self-contained, main-deck cargo handling unit. The main part of the system was carried in the lower cargo compartment and was run out

on a self-contained platform. The other structure was loaded on the main deck. It took two workers approximately 30 minutes to deploy and assemble the unit which could handle 13,000-pound loads on 125-inch by 104-inch pallets. Power for the hoist was supplied by the aircraft self-contained auxiliary power unit, connected via an external hookup.

The first Series 20 (Ship 28) made its maiden flight on February 28, piloted by George Jansen and F. E. "Phil" Blum. John Chamberlain and Joseph Tomich were the two engineers aboard. Telemetry and instrumentation – the same package as carried on Ship One – was monitored by flight-test engineer Henning Andresen. The flight lasted four hours and 10 minutes, terminating at Yuma.

The Series 20 prototype, N141US (ln 28/msn 46750). The dangling cone was used for airspeed readings in relatively undisturbed airflow.

Meanwhile, the first Series 30 (Ship 46) had already reached the wing-fuselage joining phase. Much of the testing on the Series 20 would be applicable to the Series 30, but planning called for two Series 20s and two Series 30s to be used in the flight-test certification programs.

By the end of February, only six months after the first delivery, 19 DC-10s were in service with United, American and National.

Though most marketing efforts were still concentrated on the DC-10, MDC salesmen were still discussing the DC-10 Twin with airline representatives. The design had changed very little over the previous six months except that in March, salesmen began talking to TriStar buyers about a version powered by uprated RB.211 engines. The reason behind this was Eastern Air Lines' growing attention to the European Airbus. Several other airlines showed interest, so MDC built a metal cabin mock-up of its proposed Twin and showed it to representatives from 14 airlines in mid-April. Inevitably, several airlines requested changes to the basic specification.

The European carriers, particularly those operating charter fleets, wanted increased payload and range, plus a lower price to compete with the A-300. The price was pegged at $16.2 million in 1972 dollars, with initial deliveries available in late 1974, assuming a July 1972 launch. The European carriers were being offered A-300s for $1 million less.

It should be pointed out that when new aircraft are sold, the price is quoted in the current dollars, then adjusted for inflation at the time of delivery. International aircraft sales negotiations are usually conducted using U.S.-dollar figures.

The customer list continued to grow when Venezuelan flag carrier VIASA signed for two Series 30s on April 12. These had been part of the KLM options but, since VIASA and KLM had a long history of cooperation and common equipment, it was a logical choice for the South American airline.

Continental's New Version

Continental received its first Series 10 on April 14 plus another four in the following month. The Continental models differed from earlier DC-10s in that the forward lower cargo door was larger, 104 inches by 66 inches, allowing five 88-inch by 125-inch pallets to be carried in the forward cargo hold. Earlier DC-10s had 70-inch by 66-inch openings. The larger doors became an option on all future upper-galley versions. Continental's DC-10s entered service on June 1 on the Los Angeles–Denver–Chicago route with

41 first-class and 157 coach-class seats. Following the lead of American and United, Continental installed lounges with stand-up bars in both classes. Film actress Audrey Meadows, the wife of President Robert F. Six, designed the interior decor; even the lavatories were adorned with framed pictures.

Northwest exercised eight of its 14 options for Series 20s on April 18, bringing its total to 22 firm. These, plus the last four of the initial order, were to be powered by the P&W JT9-25, rated at 50,000 pounds thrust whereas the first 10 still retained the earlier JT9-15. The announcement followed the first flight of the second Series 20, which flew in Northwest's colors a few days earlier.

Sales continued on April 24 when Continental announced that it had picked up four of the outstanding options, raising the firm order to 12, and making it the first customer for the convertible version of the Series 10F. The DC-10 announced tally now stood at 149 firm plus 73 options, from 24 airlines; unannounced orders and options brought the totals to 161 and 77, respectively.

Deliveries of the first DC-10s added significantly to corporate earnings in the fourth quarter of 1971 with the upward trend continuing in the first quarter of 1972. The outlook seemed very positive.

In May 1972, MDC used the delivery flight of United's thirteenth DC-10 for a demonstration tour to several U.S. Air Force bases before putting it on display as part of Transpo '72 at Dulles Airport in Washington, D.C. Sales presentations were made to senior officers of the Strategic Air Command and representatives of the Electronics System division of the Air Force Systems Command. During Transpo '72, United exercised seven options to bring the total buy to 32 DC-10s.

Meanwhile, the two Series 20s had racked up more than 200 flight hours and were meeting the performance predictions in a trouble-free manner.

Upgrading the Twin

After evaluating the feedback from the April mock-up visits, MDC made a number of revisions to the specification. By September, the fuselage section forward of the wing was reduced by a further three feet, but the MTOW had increased to 360,000 pounds, giving it a 2,300-mile range versus the original 1,540 miles with the same payload. Its fuel capacity was 134,500 gallons. The Twin was offered with a choice of upper or lower galleys. Maximum seating with a lower galley was 331. A normal mix would be 34 first-class (38-inch pitch) and 202 in coach (34-inch pitch). Upper galley models seated 34 first-class and 191 coach-class

Revised tail colors appear on VIASA DC-10-30 YV-137C (ln 290/msn 46982). In 1997, the pattern was revised yet again as shown below on YV-134C (ln 146/msn 46556).

Eddy Gual

passengers at the same comfort level. Calculations revealed that the Twin would have the same seat-mile cost (one cent per passenger-mile) as the DC-10-10 over ranges up to 1,750 miles.

MDC believed that Twin development costs would be comparatively inexpensive – one Wall Street estimate was less than $120 million – but despite its compatibility with both the Series 10 and Series 30, none of the airlines were willing to commit. Most American carriers thought that the DC-10-10 flexibility negated the need to rush into another variation. Eastern was the only U.S. carrier that was seriously interested in a big

Twin, but thought that the timing was too early for its needs. MDC had also targeted the charter subsidiaries of SAS, KLM and Swissair for initial sales of the DC-10 Twin.

At the time, the Airbus A300B had orders from three customers for 13 aircraft, while Lockheed held orders for 102 firm sales for its TriStar, and calculated that its break-even number was approximately 255 to 265 aircraft based on building just one model. Its first priority was to develop and sell a long-range version of the TriStar rather than to build a twin-engine model.

Wearing the original black logo markings, Continental DC-10-10 N68043 (ln 41/msn 46902) nears touchdown at Los Angeles. Below, DC-10-10 N68046 (ln 92/msn 47800) with the later red ball logo. (both Author)

In 1993, a new scheme was introduced as shown on Series 30 N68060 (ln 331/msn 47850). An Alitalia logo reflects a code-sharing agreement between the two airlines. (Roy Lock)

Former Western DC-10-10 N905WA (ln 153/msn 46938) has seen service with several small airlines, including Air Hawaii, Hawaiian Express, Capitol Airlines and Pacific East.

Hawaiian's DC-10-10s are all former American Airlines aircraft, including N122AA (ln 56/msn 46522), one of the latest used. (Author)

Key Air, a short-lived subsidiary of World Airways, operated Series 10 N917JW (ln 83/msn 46727) during the summer of 1990. (Malcolm Nason)

Leased from United in 1986, Leisure Air DC-10-10 N1826U (ln 169/msn 46625) also wears a tour operator's title. (Edwin Terbeek)

The formerly Western and Delta N902WA (ln 104/msn 46928), 5N-DGI was intended for Nigerian carrier Okada but was sold to Shabair instead. (Bob Shane)

Ex-Laker, Arrow Air DC-10-10 N902JW (ln 47/msn 46905). (Peter Samson)

Arrow Air DC-10-10 N904WA (ln 112/msn 46930) in a non-standard livery. (Author's Collection)

THY DC-10-10 TC-JAU (ln 33/msn 46705) in a 1989 paint scheme. Converted to a freighter in 1989, it became N68058 with FedEx. (Authors Collection)

Continental Micronesia leases its aircraft from parent Continental, typified by DC-10-10 N68044 (ln 43/msn 46903). (Roy Lock)

Caribbean Airways leased Laker DC-10-10 G-BBSZ (ln 83/msn 46727) during the late 1970s. (Author's Collection)

Omni Air Express operates DC-10-10s on charter services. N450AX (ln 162/msn 46942) previously served with National, Pan Am and American. (Roy Lock)

Above, ex-Western DC-10-10 N909WA (ln 252/msn 46983) flew with Scanair and Premiair as SE-DHY before being re-registered OY-CNY. Below, taken over by U.K. airline Airtours, the colors changed as shown below on DC-10-10 OY-CNT (ln 322/msn 47833).

THY subsidiary Bogazici Hava Tasimaciliti (BHT) operated two DC-10-10s, including TC-JAU (ln 33/msn 46705), on charters between 1987 and 1989. (Author's Collection)

Replacing a DC-8, Project Orbis DC-10-10 N220AU (ln 2/msn 46501) is an airborne ophthalmic teaching hospital that tours under-developed countries. (George Ditchfield)

An electronics/radar research vehicle owned by Raytheon Corp, DC-10-10 N910SF (ln 65/msn 46524) was once American Airlines N124AA. (Roy Lock)

Two ex-Laker DC-10-10s, G-BJZD (ln 269/msn 46970) and G-BJZE (ln 272/msn 46973), were bought by British Caledonian in 1982 and assigned to BCA Charter Ltd. The company was renamed Calair International in 1985 and then Novair in 1988. Both aircraft later migrated to FedEx.

Ex-Laker Series 10, G-AZZC (ln 47/msn 46905) eventually became N573SC with Sun Country. It was broken up for spares in 1997.
(Greg Drawbaugh)

National lived up to its old slogan "Airline to the Stars" by naming some DC-10s after Hollywood legends. Series 30 N82NA (ln 165/msn 46713) wore *Sammy Davis Jr.*

Shabair, a Zairian airline, leased several DC-10s between 1993-95, including Series 10 9Q-CSS (ln 104/msn 46928).
It was previously owned by Western. (via Eddy Gual)

SAS associate Scanair operated several ex-Western Series 10s, including SE-DHZ (ln 251/msn 46977), which later went to Sun Country. (Paul Bannwarth)

New operator Skyservice USA started flying in 1999 with DC-10-10 N571SC (ln 283/msn 46645). The livery is that of former operator Premiair. (Michael Carter)

In 1999, Emery Air Freight began adding converted Series 10Fs, including N68042 (ln 40/msn 46901), previously flown by Continental. (Carl Gallmeister)

The prototype Series 30 N1339U (In 46/msn 46550) rolls out of the Final Fit and Functions hangar.

The first Series DC-10-30 (Ship 46) was officially rolled out on June 1, 1972. It was timely because the last DC-8, a Series 63, had been delivered to SAS on May 17. By then, American and United each had 13 DC-10s in revenue service while Continental and National were both operating six. At Long Beach, Ship 70 had reached the wing-fuselage mating position and Laker's first DC-10, Ship 47, was already on the flight line. Four days later, AeroMexico (formerly Aeronaves de Mexico) announced that it had ordered two Series 30s.

The FAA approved the DC-10 to carry 380 passengers plus a crew of 11 on June 12. This allowed Laker and the other supplemental airlines to reconfigure the DC-10s to 10-abreast (3-4-3) seating through most of the cabin. Seat pitches were reduced from 34 inches to 31- or 32-inch spacing. FAA-controlled demonstrations showed the entire complement could be evacuated in 74 seconds, well inside the 90-second limit.

A Major Incident

While climbing through 12,000 feet en route from Detroit to Buffalo on June 13, an American Airlines DC-10 suffered cabin decompression when the aft bulk-cargo door detached from the aircraft and the rush of escaping air caused part of the aft main cabin floor to buckle. Fortunately, no one was seated in the immediate area, although two flight attendants sustained minor injuries. The collapsed floor resulted in damage to some of the elevator and rudder controls, routed in channels under the floor on either side of the aircraft center line, disabling the rudder and left elevator. In addition, the center engine shut down when its controls were damaged. The crew reduced power and returned to Detroit, controlling the aircraft with the ailerons and wing engine differential thrust. Keeping the aircraft straight on the landing rollout was difficult, but the aircraft was brought to a safe stop.

A metal coffin that fell through the cargo door opening was subsequently found near Windsor, Ontario. It was initially thought that the coffin had broken loose and crashed through the door, but further investigation centered on the latching system, even though the crew stated that no "unsafe door" warning lights had activated in the cockpit. The FAA issued a one-time inspection order covering DC-10 cargo doors, but no other discrepancies were reported. MDC advised all operators to visually check, via a small window, to be sure that the latches were properly seated

Laker DC-10-10 G-AZZC (In 47/msn 46905) being readied for delivery at Yuma. (Tim Williams)

The aft cargo door showing the latches which lock over the spools (bottom). Lock pins slide behind the latch hooks to prevent latch rotation after locking. The cage is a vent system that remains open unless the latches are properly secured, thus preventing pressurization.

after closing, and also to ensure that the warning light bulbs were working. To be on the safe side, MDC engineers began modifying the door latching mechanism and improving the cockpit warning system to give a more reliable indication of the door status.

Series 30 First Flight

Don Mullin was in command when the first Series 30, destined for KLM, made its initial flight on June 21. Jack Allavie assisted him. John Miller, who would be in command on the first MD-11 flight, rode in the observer's seat. Two flight engineers, Steve Benya and Bill Williams, were also in the cockpit. The standard telemetry and recording devices were monitored by flight-test engineer Les Spengler.

The flight lasted 5 hours and 25 minutes, reaching a speed of Mach 0.88 at 35,000 feet. Two coupled approach and landing cycles were made at Long Beach. Reaching such a high point in the flight envelope on the first

flight was based on the experience gained during the 300 hours of testing already conducted on Series 20 aircraft. Part of the trials included use of a new Mark II area navigation system (R-Nav) that a number of DC-10 customers had selected.

By mid-July, the two Series 20s had logged more than 368 of the 550 flying hours required by the FAA. On July 13, one aircraft took off at a MTOW of 565,000 pounds, 10,000 pounds over the design limit. It landed weighing 549,000 pounds as part of the rejected takeoff braking trials. The normal landing weight was 411,000 pounds. In its first month, the Series 30 flew more than 43 of the planned 250 hours.

Around The World

An around-the-world sales tour began on July 21, 1972, when a DC-10-10, named *Friendship '72* and piloted by Don Mullin, headed for its first stop at Vancouver, British Columbia in Canada. Interestingly, the aircraft passed through Tokyo just one week after a TriStar had called, on a similar tour. Airport officials conducted noise measurements on both types and concluded that there was no discernible difference between the two aircraft. In all, the DC-10 visited 37 locations in 19 countries. It flew 32,725 miles in 25 days while accumulating 101 flight hours and carrying more than 5,500 people on demonstration flights. During the tour, MDC officials revealed that the DC-10 order book stood at 168 firm plus 62 options from 25 airlines.

The DC-10 Twin was also strongly marketed in the Japan discussions. Mitsubishi approached MDC to discuss a joint venture to build the aircraft while Lockheed tried to complete a similar agreement with Nihon Aeroplane Manufacturing Company. But neither project gained enough support from the Japanese government to proceed. By then, MDC had invested $7 million in the project and determined that a minimum order of 50 aircraft would be required to commit to production.

Just one year after the DC-10 entered service, 42 aircraft had been delivered, all to domestic airlines. Performance had exceeded design expectations with shorter field lengths, higher initial cruising altitudes and excellent overall serviceability. The only problems encountered were oil leaks from the center engine crank cases. In two cases, oil starvation caused partial breakup of the engine but its location prevented damage to the rest of the airframe. GE and MDC identified the problem and beefed up the support structure; operating procedures were also revised.

The Lounge Debate

After one year of service, the merit of lounges on U.S. domestic coach-class flights became the subject of review by the airlines. National had operated successfully without the feature and Delta, which was about to initiate DC-10 service, said it couldn't see removing 40 revenue seats and adding cabin staff to support the lounges. Its view was that the CAB should allow it to reduce seat prices by 15 percent on routes where it was competing with lounge-equipped aircraft. This was in the era when the airlines had no freedom to change prices or seating layouts without CAB approval. American, Continental and United all contended that the lounges still served as a useful attraction and, as the flights were still flying less than full, the seats would have been empty in any case.

Eastern and TWA both inaugurated TriStar service with lounges installed. When Eastern removed them from one of its initial six L-1011s, it was deluged with complaints. However, lounges began to disappear from the coach sections of both the DC-10s and TriStars as traffic improved.

The first Series 30 lifts off on June 21 1972. (Author)

Elegant
First Class
Lounge

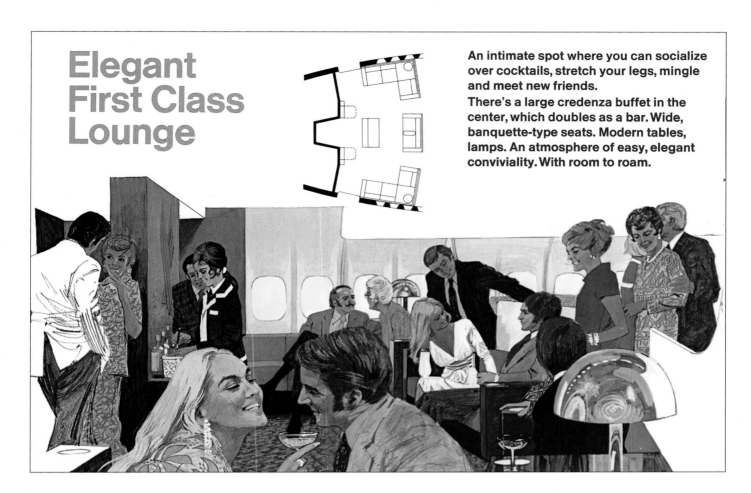

An intimate spot where you can socialize over cocktails, stretch your legs, mingle and meet new friends.

There's a large credenza buffet in the center, which doubles as a bar. Wide, banquette-type seats. Modern tables, lamps. An atmosphere of easy, elegant conviviality. With room to roam.

Luxurious
Coach
Lounge

Another American innovation, our coach lounge is a place to enjoy the freedom and sociability that extra space allows.

Bigger than most living rooms, it seats 11 passengers and easily accommodates about a dozen more. Wall to wall comfort, 19 feet wide, with a circular stand-up bar.

American Airlines' DC-10 forward first-class and aft coach-class lounges are depicted in an early sales brochure. (Jon Proctor Collection)

One of the aircraft bought by United and leased to Delta because of delayed TriStar deliveries, DC-10-10 N603DA (ln 67/msn 47967) climbs out from New York's La Guardia Airport. (Jon Proctor)

More Orders

The fall brought a small flurry of announced orders for DC-10s. The first was from Continental Airlines, which picked up the four remaining options for DC-10-10CFs on September 20. Three days later, Turkish Airlines (THY) purchased three of the former Mitsui aircraft, all to be delivered by February 1973. SAS announced the conversion of three options to firm buys on October 3, and kept the three remaining options. Due to inflation, the price edged up to $22 million each for 1975 deliveries. Delta Air Lines accepted its first DC-10-10 on October 11 and took it to Yuma for crew training flights before heading to Atlanta. The 50th DC-10, American's 22nd aircraft, was handed over on October 20.

The FAA issued a provisional type certificate for the Series 40 on October 4, thus allowing delivery to Northwest Airlines for route proving and pilot training. Flight testing had reached 576 hours by this time. The type designation had been changed from Series 20 to Series 40 in response to Northwest's Donald Nyrop, who argued that the aircraft was much improved over the original design and he wanted to advertise that he had the latest version of the DC-10. Similar gamesmanship had taken place between airlines during the early days of both the DC-8 and DC-9.

Meanwhile, the second Northwest aircraft was used to establish point-to-point records as part of the final function and reliability flights for full certification. On October 9, it covered the 6,600 miles between Long Beach and Hong Kong in 14 hours and 44 minutes against headwinds. After a visit to Tokyo, the Series 40 continued on to Hawaii. Next, it flew from Honolulu to Buenos Aires, a distance of 6,725 miles, in 14 hours and 8 minutes. A third record was established on October 14 with an 11-hour and 52-minute flight from Rio de Janeiro to Long Beach, a distance of 6,616 miles.

Northwest DC-10-40 N142US (ln 36/msn 46751) departing from Long Beach on a June 1973 test flight.

Several records were captured by Northwest DC-10-40 N143US (ln 53/msn 46752) seen at Buenos Aires.

The FAA issued the Series 40 type certificate on October 27. Slightly less than 600 hours had been flown during the certification process. The first aircraft was delivered to Northwest on November 10, a morale booster for Northwest; its pilots had just returned on October 2 after a three-month strike against the airline. The first service was flown between Minneapolis and Tampa via Milwaukee on December 13.

On October 25, another major milestone was achieved when the British Civil Aviation Authority (CAA) issued an airworthiness and type certificate for the DC-10-10, which was about to enter service with Laker Airways. Freddie Laker accepted the first aircraft the following day with the second following just three weeks later. It was less than a month since he had actually signed the purchase agreement with Mitsui. The timing for this had been predicated on receiving CAA approval for Skytrain services just a few days earlier. However, a long battle followed before Skytrain flights actually began.

The first revenue service was a charter flight from London-Gatwick to Palma, Majorca on November 21, making Laker the first foreign DC-10 operator.

Structural Testing Completed

In addition to the initial structural testing carried out on Ship Two, three sets of DC-10 structures were separately subjected to load cycles which equaled 84,000 flights and 120,000 flight hours. Included were cockpit-forward fuselage, center section-wing and rear fuselage-empennage sections. These components were the fourth set of production structures to be built. Breaking the aircraft into three components reduced the amount of downtime for inspections.

Computers varied the pressurization and loading to simulate all types of operations, including the occasional hard landing, turbulence and similar anomalies. In a number of cases, minor failures occurred during the course of the tests and additional supporting material was installed. The failures all occurred prior to any deliveries, so changes were incorporated before service entry. The program took 19 months to complete and was concluded in mid-October at a cost of $30 million.

Northwest has purchased several used DC-10-30s for long-haul services. N211NW (ln 171/msn 46868) wears the name *City of Amsterdam*. (Greg Drawbaugh)

Challenge Air Cargo's DC-10-40F N140WE (ln 212/msn 46920) was the first of the former JAL aircraft to be converted to a freighter. (Michael Bolden)

Jet 24 leased two ex-NWA Series 40s from Boeing in 1984-85. N144US (ln 66/msn 46753) was re-registered N144JW during its short sublease to Air Panama in 1985. (Author's Collection)

N142US (ln 36/msn 46751) was traded to Boeing by Northwest and then sold to American Trans Air. (via Eddy Gual)

Japan Asia is a JAL company formed to serve Taiwan only. DC-10-40s JA8535 (ln 230/msn 46662) and JA8532 (ln 220/msn 46660) represent two schemes that have been used.

Japan Air Charter (JAZ) is a charter subsidiary of Japan Airlines. DC-10-40 JA8544 (ln 340/msn 47852) appears in an early livery. (Author's Collection)

Chapter X
SERIES 30 INTO SERVICE

Air Zaire was the second African airline to receive DC-10-30s, taking delivery of 9Q-CLI (ln 90/msn 47886) in September 1973. It has been stored since 1995 because of political problems in Zaire.

The FAA issued the Series 30 type certificate on November 21, 1972, just five months after the first flight. Two aircraft participated in the flight test program, logging 368 hours and 35 minutes during 265 flights. The handing over of the first Series 30s to representatives of the KSSU group immediately followed a certification ceremony. KLM and Swissair each took one aircraft. UTA's first DC-10-30 was present but not yet ready for delivery, while the first SAS aircraft was not scheduled for delivery until late 1974.

The 27th customer, VARIG Airlines of Brazil, ordered two DC-10-30s and took two options on November 30. The first DC-10-10 for THY was handed over on December 7 and entered service in time for the holiday rush.

Swissair launched the first scheduled DC-10 service across the Atlantic on December 15, between Zurich, Montreal and Chicago. The inaugural occurred just one week after the aircraft had been delivered nonstop from Long Beach to Zurich in 10 hours and one minute. The airline also announced its purchase of a seventh DC-10 for February 1975 delivery.

Twin Studies Continue

At its year-end quarterly meeting, the MDC board of directors approved an additional $4 million be spent for production engineering of the Twin. This was probably prompted by the first flight of the Airbus A300B on October 28, along with Boeing's increased 727-200 production rate. The Boeing tri-jet was aiming at the same market niche. Another factor was Swissair's growing need to replace its DC-9-30s with a larger aircraft. Other KSSU members, plus Atlantis and Iberia also indicated interest.

In the United States, Delta, Allegheny and Eastern were the main targets for near-term sales, with American, United and TWA considered as longer-term potential customers. For the U.S. airlines, the Twin's multi-stop capability over short sectors without refueling was the main attraction. The aircraft's maximum landing weight was only 12,000 pounds less than its MTOW.

The Twin design stabilized with a span of 161 feet, 4 inches, a length of 168 feet and height of 57 feet, 7 inches. Several other studies included

fuselage lengths between 140 feet and 182 feet, with seating ranging from 197 to 302. In addition to the CF6-50C, the Pratt & Whitney JT9D-57 – rated at 52,000 pounds of thrust – was being offered. The standard mixed class configuration was 28 in first-class with 38-inch pitched (2-2-2) seating and 211 in coach-class in a 2-4-2 arrangement at a 34-inch pitch. The MTOW stood at 340,000 pounds with a fuel capacity of 230,000 pounds.

The company's goal was to win orders from enough airlines – particularly U.S. carriers – to make preliminary commitments prior to the April 1973 board meeting. Certification was planned for September 1975 with deliveries commencing shortly thereafter.

Switched Aircraft

In early December 1972, the first two DC-10s exchanged identities. Initially, Ship One had been fittingly registered as N10DC and Ship Two wore N101AA to reflect its planned delivery to American Airlines. However, Ship Two was still completing autoland trials as its contractual delivery date approached. Ship One had finished its test program, so an agreement was reached to refurbish it for delivery it to American as N101AA to keep American's fleet sequence unsullied. Accordingly, Ship Two was re-registered as N10DC and remained with MDC until it was sold to Laker Airways in June 1977.

The year ended on a mixed note when, on December 21, Lufthansa announced its conversion of five previously unannounced options to firm buys, bringing its fleet order to nine DC-10-30s. Sales then totaled 184 firm orders plus 44 options. Sixty-two aircraft had been delivered to 10 airlines. However, American canceled its remaining 11 options for DC-10s, citing the lack of predicted traffic growth,

Air New Zealand accepted its first DC-10-30 on January 11, 1973, which headed for Auckland via Honolulu on January 22 following crew training at Yuma and a short wait for passenger seats, a common problem at the time. Service began on February 3 between Auckland and Sydney; flights to Los Angeles started on April 2.

National ordered five more Series 10s and two Series 30s on January 29, raising its total order to 14 Series 10s and four Series 30s.

Offsetting this order, AeroMexico postponed the conversion of its two options on January 31, but purchased six DC-9-30s instead. Air Zaire contracted for two Series 30s on February 7. After delivery on February 18, UTA's first DC-10-30 flew nonstop to Paris from Yuma, Arizona in nine hours and 41 minutes.

Series 30F First Flight

ONA's first convertible DC-10 undertook its maiden flight on March 1, lasting just over four hours. Project pilot Phil Blum was in command, assisted by A. P. Johnson and flight engineer John Chamberlain with David Houle as flight-test engineer. The aircraft landed at Yuma, where most of the test flying would be based. On the following day, Air Afrique's first DC-10-30 flew nonstop from Long Beach to Dakar, Senegal on its delivery flight.

First ATLAS Deliveries

Western increased its order for DC-10-10s to six on March 21, following the CAB's rejection of the proposed American-Western merger. On that same day, the first Series 30s were formally handed over to Alitalia and Iberia at a joint ceremony. Actually, it was Alitalia's second aircraft; the first had been delivered without fanfare on February 6 and flown to Yuma for crew training. The second aircraft left Long Beach the following day to fly nonstop to Rome in 11 hours and 32 minutes, covering 5,575 miles.

Iberia's DC-10 had two specially commissioned original paintings by Salvador Dali mounted on bulkheads in the passenger cabins as part of a $70,000 contract with Dali to design the interior decor of the new aircraft. The March 28 delivery flight, to Gerona, Spain, established a sixth record for the DC-10 when it flew the 5,475-mile segment from Long Beach in 10 hours and 47 minutes.

During the visit to Long Beach by Alitalia's management, negotiations were completed for another four Series 30s, bringing the firm total to eight with one option remaining. The announcement was made on April 1. Two days later, Iberia converted two options, bringing its total firm orders to five.

Series 30F Type Certificate

The FAA issued a type certificate for the DC-10-30F on April 13, followed three days later by a joint delivery ceremony for Overseas National and Trans International. Both airlines had 345-seat interiors with movie and stereo installations, a first for charter aircraft. At this time, MDC began referring to these models as DC-10-30CFs.

TIA's first widebody all-cargo service commenced on April 30 with a flight from Oakland, California to Hong Kong. Upon returning, the aircraft was re-configured for passenger use and flew to London-Gatwick on May 4, making TIA the first U.S. supplemental airline to operate widebody charter services. ONA used the return leg of a proving flight from Los Angeles to London-Gatwick as a revenue segment on May 6, edging out World Airways' Boeing 747-273C introduction on May 12. In the first month of operation, TIA's DC-10 amassed 396 hours and ONA accumulated approximately 350 hours flying with its new aircraft.

TIA reported that transforming the aircraft from cargo to passenger configuration took longer than anticipated, mainly due to reinstallation of the upper galley components and the seat track wiring for the audio systems. However, since cargo flying would be concentrated in the winter months and passenger flying in the summer, reconfiguring would be kept to a minimum.

By the end of April 1973, DC-10 firm orders stood at 195 plus eight classed as "contingent firm," or subject to completion of financing, plus 25 options for a total of 228. Eighty-seven aircraft had been delivered. Pakistan International Airlines (PIA) purchased three Series 30s on June 2 with two deliveries set for 1974 and one for 1975. Deposits were also placed for three options. This sale brought the total to 28 customers including some unannounced buyers. Among them was Philippine Airlines, which was in the process of buying two Series 30s.

On June 8, the 100th DC-10 – a Series 30 for Air Zaire – was delivered. Three days later, National received its first Series 30.

The Board Decision

When the MDC board held its July meeting, no orders had been placed for the Twin, and Airbus Industrie not been very successful in selling the A-300B. Meanwhile, Swissair had recently elected to postpone its widebody twin acquisition, instead becoming the launch customer for the DC-9-50 with an order for 10 aircraft. In spite of this, MDC's board allowed the continuance of the Twin program, deferring the final decision until its October meeting. The consensus was that the market would be ready in 1980. Following this decision, Jackson McGowen announced his retirement as president, citing health as the basis for his decision. McGowen was succeeded by John Brizendine, who promptly named William T. Gross as his deputy.

Competition Increases

Meanwhile, Lockheed was developing the L-1011-2 with an intended range of 4,000 miles and a 272-passenger capacity. Its dimensions matched the earlier version, but with a stronger structure and the addition of a center section 30,000-pound fuel tank. Its Rolls-Royce RB.211-24 engines were rated at 45,000 pounds of thrust. Potential airline customers included British Airways (BA), which had recently ordered six TriStar 1s for its European division, plus Air Canada and Pan American. BA's long-haul division and some Middle Eastern carriers were also on the list because this version could reach most European cities from New York.

Although the Series 30 still seemed to be sweeping the board in its class, competition was beginning to surface from another direction. Boeing was concerned that the DC-10 was eating into the lower end of its widebody market and decided to reevaluate its situation. As mentioned earlier, the Seattle company had considered both a tri-jet version of the Boeing 747 and widebody twins. In early 1973, a series of studies and wind tunnel tests were carried out on a shortened version of the 747. The go-ahead to proceed was given in June 1973 under the title of "Boeing 747 Short Body" (747SB), later changed to 747 Special Performance (747SP) when Pan American announced an order for 10 firm plus 15 options in

In December 1972, unfinished flight testing and American's delivery contract led MDC to swap registrations between Ship One and Ship Two (msn 46501), seen here as N10DC. (Author's Collection)

VARIG, Brazil's flag airline, still has DC-10-30s in service after 25 years. Above, PP-VMQ (ln 176/msn 46941) appears in delivery markings.
In 1998, VARIG restyled its colors as depicted below by PP-VMB (ln 156/msn 46945) and PP-VMU (ln 332/msn 47842), converted to all cargo.

Less than nine months after delivery, Iberia DC-10-30 EC-CBN (ln 87/msn 46925) was destroyed in an undershot approach to Boston in December 1973.

Series 30 EC-CBP (ln 100/msn 46927) wears the paint scheme Iberia introduced in 1969. (via Eddy Gual)

September 1973. The Pan Am specification was for a 6,000-mile range with 200 mixed-class passengers. MDC had offered a DC-10-30LR with increased fuel capacity to provide a range of 5,600 miles with a full load, while Lockheed proposed an L-1011-2LR which traded seats for more fuel while retaining the same dimensions and weights as the L-1011-2.

Europe's First Widebody Convertible

SABENA formally took delivery of its first Series 30F on September 21. The interior layout selected was unusual with the first-class section located aft of the cargo door, allowing four pallets to be loaded in the forward section. Total seating was 187. Following crew training, the aircraft remained grounded in Brussels for more than two months due to a pay dispute between pilots and management. Later, the DC-10s were mainly allocated to African and Asian services.

AeroMexico received approval to purchase two Series 30s on October 19, with deliveries scheduled for April and May 1974. Service was scheduled to commence on the Acapulco–Mexico City–New York route on May 1. Delivery of the second aircraft would allow trans-Atlantic operations by mid-May with services to Madrid and Paris via Miami.

One of the annoying problems encountered with the introduction of large aircraft was the limited amount of carry-on baggage stowage space. This was compounded as higher-density economy-class seating was introduced. To address the problem, MDC in October built a new mock-up with centerline storage bins suspended from the ceiling. Among the first interested customers were members of the KSSU Group. These center racks became standard and were retrofitted to all DC-10s.

Engine Problems

A National DC-10 suffered a freak accident on November 3 while flying at 30,000 feet over Albuquerque, New Mexico. The front inlet cowling of the right wing engine detached and struck the exposed engine causing it to disintegrate. Unfortunately, several blades punctured the cabin and caused decompression. One blade took out a passenger window completely and a passenger was sucked out of the cabin in spite of the fact that he wearing a seat belt. Apart from the engine, the wing leading edge also suffered severe damage. The crew made an emergency descent and safe landing at Albuquerque.

Super DC-10s on Offer

On November 6, MDC announced several new versions of the DC-10. The first was the Ultra-Long-Range (ULR) aircraft, a standard DC-10-30 airframe with an increased MTOW of 580,000 pounds. An all-freighter version of the Series 30 with an MTOW of 572,000 pounds would be capable of carrying 180,000 pounds of cargo on trans-Atlantic flights.

But the most interesting was an offer to stretch the DC-10 either 25 feet or 40 feet with a 1977 delivery schedule. The aircraft, called Super DC-10s, could seat between 28 percent and 40 percent more passengers than existing models. The uprated CF6-50F engine rated at 52,500 pounds of thrust would power the new models. The all-freighter was also offered with Pratt & Whitney JT9D-59s producing a similar thrust rating.

MDC Chairman Emeritus Donald Douglas Sr. presided at the hand-over ceremony of Lufthansa's first Series 30 on November 12. The following day, Martinair accepted its first Series 30CF, fitted out with 371 seats. Late in December, while positioning for a series of Hadj flights, Martinair's DC-10 flew the 6,850-mile segment from Amsterdam to Djakarta, Indonesia nonstop in 13 hours and 45 minutes. It landed with more than 10 tons of fuel remaining. This was the longest DC-10 flight to date.

At the year-end, MDC had 235 DC-10 orders and options of which 125 had been delivered. Due to the continuing fuel crisis created by OPEC, only 22 aircraft had been sold during the year. The production rate had been running at about 0.71 per week, but plans were in hand to increase the rate in 1974 to one per week.

Artist's impression of the ultra-long-range DC-10.

PIA'S DC-10-30 AP-AXE (ln 172/msn 46935) was destroyed in a February 1981 hangar fire. (Author's Collection)

Later PIA deliveries had the stars removed. The final scheme, introduced in 1976, is worn by Series 30 AP-AYM (ln 229/msn 47889).

AeroCancun's DC-10-15 XA-TDI (ln 357/msn 48259) was previously with Mexicana. (Bob Shane)

Aero Lyon leased DC-10-30 F-BTDD (ln 244/msn 46963) from UTA in 1997. It was later sold to AOM. (Avimage)

Still wearing basic AeroMexico livery, Aero Peru DC-10-15 N10045 (ln 357/msn 48259) appears in January 1994. (via Eddy Gual)

Kenyan airline African Safari operates ex-KLM DC-10-30 5Y-MBA (ln 185/msn 46952) on charter flights from Europe. (Paul Bannwarth)

DC-10-30 N524MD (ln 289/msn 46999) was leased to Aeroflot by MDC from 1995 to 1999. It was built for SIA. (Malcolm Nason)

Ex-UTA, Air Europe leased Series 30 OO-JOT (ln 63/msn 46850) from Challenge Air Cargo during the winter months of 1995-96. (Paul Bannwarth)

When UTA and Air France merged in December 1992, one DC-10-30 N54649 (ln 193/msn 46854) operated briefly in AF colors. (Avimage)

Air Florida operated with several different color schemes at the same time. Shown are DC-10-30CF's N101TV (ln 96/msn 46800) and N1035F (ln 257/msn 46992). (both Bruce Drum)

As a private company, Air Liberte operated its fleet, including DC-10-30 N345HC (ln 345/msn 48265) in these simple colors. After becoming part of British Airways, new markings were created, as seen below on Series 30 F-GPVA (ln 181/msn 47956).

Minerve operated services for Air Guadeloupe and Air Martinique using DC-10-30 F-GGMZ (ln 260/msn 46990), painting the aircraft differently on each side. (via Eddy Gual)

French charter company Air Outre Mer operated several DC-10-30s, including F-ODLX (In 233/msn 46872). (Bernard Kergal)

In 1992, Air Outre Mer changed its name to AOM French Airlines after a merger with Minerve. F-GNDC (In 213/msn 47849) appears with revised titles. (Paul Bannwarth)

Air Pacific is one of several airlines to have leased Series 30 N821L (In 136/msn 47848) from ILFC. It was built for Air New Zealand. (Author's Collection)

Wearing test registration N54643 (In 125/msn 47887), this DC-10-30 became HS-VGE with Air Siam. It crashed at Tripoli, Libya in July 1989 while owned by Korean Air.

The year 1974 got off to a good start with VARIG's order for its fourth Series 30 on January 8. But the big news came six days later, when JAL bought six DC-10-40s powered by P&W JT9D-53As rated at 53,000 pounds thrust. Deliveries were to commence in early 1976. KLM picked up a seventh Series 30 on February 11. A day later, Air New Zealand (ANZ) purchased three Series 30s, bringing its fleet to six. The reason for its order was a proposed interchange service with British Airways (BA) whereby ANZ's DC-10s would operate on BA's Los Angeles–London segments. The flights would be operated by BA crews as an extension of ANZ's Auckland–Los Angeles service. PIA's DC-10 delivered on March 1, the first destined for an Asian airline.

The Paris Crash

While climbing out from Paris-Orly Airport on March 3, THY's DC-10-10 TC-JAV suffered a rapid cabin decompression and loss of power. At 12,000 feet, the aircraft immediately initiated a partial roll onto a new heading and rapidly descended to crash in a heavily wooded area near Ermenonville. There were no survivors among the 11 crew and 335 passengers. The discovery of six seats and their occupants plus the rear cargo door some nine miles from the main crash site quickly pointed to the primary accident cause.

Investigators determined that the door had separated because it had been improperly latched. The door-mounted hooks had failed to engage the fixed pins properly, and the additional heavy force used to close the external latch handle merely resulted in bent internal rods and tubes without locking the door securely. The automatic venting system activated by the latch mechanism was connected to the latch handle, not the latch pins, so it failed to activate.

Normally, a force of just eight pounds was required to close the latches. Tests showed that the ground handler at Orly had applied some 250 pounds pressure to force the latch closed. Unfortunately, the modification to require a force of 440 pounds had not been incorporated nor had a closed-loop system been installed. This system would not have allowed the vent to close (thereby preventing the cabin pressurizing) unless the latches were properly secured. It was later revealed that these modifications, designed after American's Detroit incident, had not been incorporated, even though company records indicated the changes had been made.

After this accident, the FAA mandated that all widebody transports must be capable of withstanding lower-deck decompressions through openings of at least 20 square feet. Operators were given the option of strengthening the cabin floor or having an enlarged upper-lower deck venting system. All in-service aircraft were required to be compliant by December 1977. MDC, having begun design efforts immediately after the accident, incorporated both methods. Some

The ill-fated THY DC-10-10 TC-JAV (In 29/msn 46704) on a pre-delivery test flight.

In 1989, JAL abandoned the traditional fuselage cheatline shown above on DC-10-40 JA8530 (ln 212/msn 46920) for the contemporary, plain livery seen below.

thought was given to re-routing all the engine and empennage control systems above the cabin ceiling, but this was dropped in favor of the simpler venting changes.

Humming Along

In spite of the publicity surrounding the Paris accident, the pace of events at Long Beach remained high. VIASA accepted its first DC-10-30 – part of the KLM batch – on April 3. Next, Western took delivery of its first DC-10 on April 19 and initiated service from Minneapolis to Honolulu via Los Angeles on June 16. VARIG's first Series 30 was handed over on May 29 and entered trans-Atlantic service on June 24.

Just prior to SABENA receiving its second DC-10-30CF on June 10, the Export-Import Bank gave some indication of current DC-10 prices by announcing that it would contribute just over $6 million of the $22.45 million price for a June delivery. UTA increased its DC-10 fleet to six with an order for one on June 12. Korean received its first Series 30 on June 20. June 27 saw another KLM aircraft delivered, but this time in the colors of Philippine Airlines on a long-term lease.

The Philippine Airlines DC-10 was seized by the U.S. government at San Francisco on July 26 due to a dispute over capacity rights between the two countries. The aircraft was released following an interim agreement reached on August 12. The airline was fined $267,000 and later sued to recover the money.

On August 5, the third anniversary of DC-10 service, 158 aircraft had been delivered to 28 airlines. The fleet had jointly accumulated 609,000 flight hours since entering service.

In its original livery, Korean Air Lines DC-10-30 HL-7315 (ln 160/msn 46934).

KAL's trading name changed in 1984 to Korean Air and led to a revised scheme shown on Series 30 HL-7316 (ln 188/msn 46912). (Author's Collection)

The Cockpit View

During late August, American introduced a new video cassette system to its DC-10 In Flight Entertainment (IFE) equipment, replacing the old reel-to-reel system. But the biggest innovation was the introduction of a camera located behind the pilots that was turned on during takeoffs and landings to give passengers a view through the cockpit windows. An audio system also enabled passengers to listen to the crew conversations with air traffic controllers.

White Tails

Martinair ordered a second DC-10-30CF on September 2, just one day before Air Siam signed for a "white tail" Series 30, previously built for Atlantis and stored. It was delivered on November 25 and quickly put into service on the Bangkok–Los Angeles route. In October, China Airlines (CAL) became the 34th DC-10 airline customer with an order for two Series 30s slated for early 1975 delivery. However, the Taiwanese government refused to sanction the sale just prior to delivery of the first aircraft, also built for Atlantis and stored. Painted in CAL's colors, it was flown to Yuma for further storage in March 1975 before becoming the first DC-10 delivered to British Caledonian Airways in March 1977.

Proposed New Models

At the beginning of October, MDC began making formal offers of all-freighter DC-10 models. Designated DC-10-30AF and -40AF depending on engine choice, both offered similar payload and range performance. The Dash 30AF, powered by GE CF6-50J engines rated at 54,000 pounds of thrust, had a new MTOW of 580,000 pounds and a maximum landing weight of 440,000 pounds. It could carry a 182,000-pound payload 3,500 miles.

The Series 40AF, with P&W JT9D-59As rated at 53,000 pounds thrust, had a similar range with 178,000 pounds of cargo. Both models incorporated a redesigned cargo floor and modifications that reduced drag by 3 percent. The main cargo door was totally redesigned, with the top hinge line nearly on the aircraft's centerline, allowing cargo to be loaded by overhead crane. The standard door width remained 140 inches, but an alternate 215-inch-wide door was on option. However, no sales of these versions were ever made.

The various stretched proposals all looked similar but varied considerably in performance. This impression is a 40-foot stretch.

The undelivered China Air Lines DC-10-30 N54643 (ln 179/msn 46949) was stored at Yuma for two years before going to British Caledonian as G-BEBM. (Gerry Markgraf)

During the year, several European airlines entertained a larger version, although U.S. domestic carriers showed little interest. Using the latest weights and engines specified for standard DC-10-30s, engineers updated the stretched studies with 30-foot, 40-foot and 50-foot fuselage growths. MDC's initial preference was to concentrate on the 30-foot stretch to minimize development costs. Drag improvements generated by a new wing fillet, reduced spoiler-flap gaps and modified aileron droop were expected to yield an almost 4 percent gain in performance. The rear underside profile was redesigned to maintain adequate ground clearance during rotation. The center engine thrust reverser was also eliminated. Maximum cruise altitude was reduced to 42,000 feet from 45,000 feet due to the higher weights. Inserting a 140-inch plug ahead of the wing and a 220-inch plug behind it created the 30-foot stretch. Capacity was to be 24 first-class passengers at a 40-inch pitch plus 338 in economy-class, nine-abreast at a 34-inch pitch. Also featured was a larger cargo door for the rear belly cargo hold, designed to accommodate LD-3 containers. With three GE CF6-50J engines and passengers and baggage only (a 75,000-pound load), it had a range of 4,550 miles. Carrying a maximum payload of 120,000 pounds, the predicted range was 3,400 miles. Slightly less performance was available if either the GE CF6-50C or P&W JT9D-59A power plants were selected.

Leased from KLM, Philippine Air Lines DC-10-30 PH-DTK (ln 195/msn 46914) in a typical DC-10 takeoff attitude. Below, RPC-2003 (ln 232/msn 46958) reflects the all-too-common white scheme of the '90s.

Malaysian Airline System (MAS) amended its livery several times; DC-10-30 9M-MAS (ln 228/msn 46955) illustrates two variations.

Paul Bannwarth

Cargo operations for Malaysian are carried out by MASkargo, using DC-10-30CFs leased from World Airways. Shown is N105WA (ln 127/msn 46891). (Mike Rathke)

DC-10-30 N8708Q (ln 204/msn 46892) was sold to Air Afrique as TU-TAM, but leased new to Thai Airways and eventually registered HS-TGB.

The 40-foot stretch could carry 385 passengers in a similar configuration to the shorter version. A small increase in the operating empty weight slightly reduced range.

Revised Break-even

To bolster sales efforts, MDC leased a DC-10 from Alitalia for demonstration flights in the Middle East and Africa during November. PIA subsequently announced the purchase of a fourth DC-10 at the end of the following March. The year ended with Malaysian Airlines purchasing two Series 30s on December 18.

The worldwide general recession still showed little sign of improving so, at the financial year-end, the board of directors adjusted the break-even sales point to 400 DC-10s. Earlier, the estimate had been based on 500 aircraft sold to recover the design, development and tooling costs. A direct result of this was a substantial write-off of some development costs against current earnings. At the time, Boeing was using a figure of 400 aircraft, and Lockheed had a 300 aircraft break-even number in their respective cost calculations.

In March 1975, The FAA approved the Series 10 and 30 for auto-landings under Category II conditions that allowed 1,200-foot runway visibility. The Series 40, still undergoing flight trials with the system, was approved at the beginning of May.

Thai International Airways leased two DC-10-30s and put the first one into service on April 1 between Bangkok, Frankfurt and Copenhagen. The leases were arranged through UTA, although the first aircraft was a new aircraft originally destined for Air Afrique. By the end of April, the DC-10 fleet of 190 had topped 1 million flight hours. U.S. domestic operations accounted for 111 aircraft. Seventy-nine TriStars and 98 Boeing 747s were in use by this time.

BA-ANZ Interchange

The Air New Zealand-British Airways DC-10 interchange service from Los Angeles to London began on May 7. The external markings remained in ANZ's colors; inside the cabin, BA crews transformed the aircraft with its own head rest covers, menus, utensils, glasses, napkins and other service items. A small sticker placed inside the doors announced that it was a BA flight. The timing of the new service was ideal since British Caledonian's Boeing 707 and Pan Am's Boeing 747 services had recently terminated on this route.

Lufthansa purchased a 10th Series 30 on May 12. The 200th DC-10, a series 30, was handed over to National on June 21. The next sale did not come until Martinair picked up a position previously optioned by UTA on August 25, for delivery in late 1976.

Meanwhile, the first JAL Series 40 completed its first flight on July 25, just three weeks after the Boeing 747SP's maiden flight. Flown by Cliff

Stout and Fred Blum, the Series 40 flight lasted four hours and 55 minutes. With the uprated engines, JAL's DC-10s had an MTOW of 572,000 pounds. They were also the first to specify a pod to ferry a spare power plant inboard of the left engine.

The BA Competition

Sales efforts began in earnest to interest BA in a Rolls-Royce RB.211-524-powered model re-designated as the DC-10-50. The competition was a proposed shortened TriStar Series 500, and the Boeing 747SP. As the summer progressed, MDC continued to refine its offers. A new version, the DC-10-30R was introduced with an increased MTOW of 572,000 pounds powered by 50,000-pound thrust RB.211-524B engines that would permit ranges of 5,000 miles to be flown with a full payload. Because the total order was believed to be at least 20 aircraft with an initial requirement for 12, MDC took the unusual step of offering to fund 70 percent of the engineering development costs associated with installation of the Rolls engine. Another part of the MDC offer was a large offset manufacturing contract. Aside from the engine, the new nacelle and pylons plus all-British avionics and other work would account for some 30 percent of the aircraft price. The nacelles would have been built by BAC and the pylons by Shorts of Belfast, Ireland. Over a 10-year period, the package had an estimated value of $950 million, based on worldwide sales of the DC-10-50 reaching 100.

The BA order was subsequently lost because Lockheed, under new chairmanship, had managed to escape its financial problems and the airline was able to switch existing TriStar options to the new model without adding another type to its fleet. Hence, MDC ceased work on the Rolls-Royce engine option in August.

Ironically, BA acquired eight DC-10-30s when it merged with British Caledonian in 1988, and operated the type for 11 years. The six TriStar 500s, delivered in 1979 and 1980, were all withdrawn from service in 1983 and sold to the Royal Air Force for transport use and modification into aerial refueling tankers.

Drag Improvements

In October 1974, MDC began modifying Ship Two in an effort to reduce fuel burn rates by up to five percent. The main change was a redesign of the wing root and horizontal tail fairings plus a reshaped tail cone. Other changes included minimizing the gaps between control surfaces and the wing.

Because of slow sales, MDC announced in mid-October that it would offer 10 DC-10s with a $6-million price reduction provided the customers signed for them before the end of the year, though this was later extended to January 31, 1976. All would be scheduled for 1977 delivery. The company calculated that it was cheaper than shutting down the line and re-opening it

The DC-X-200

In mid-August 1976, MDC announced the cessation of work on the DC-10 Twin as it no longer suited the market. Most airline managers felt that it was too big, with 260 seats versus 240 on the A-300B. Market indications were that an aircraft sized somewhere between the Boeing 727-200 and the A-300B would be more appropriate.

As usual, MDC's advanced design engineers started looking at several alternative designs for the new requirement. In 1974, a few engineers had been assigned to investigate new technologies for the next-generation airliner. From these efforts, the super-critical wing emerged as the best option for what was known as the Advanced Medium-Range Aircraft (AMRA).

Initially, a completely new design was proposed. The choice of power plants was numerous, and many trade-off studies included three- as well as twin-engine models, depending on the engine thrust. In general, the twin studies retained the CF6-50C engines and featured seven-abreast (2-3-2) seating. For a short time, tri-jets (D-969M series) powered by P&W JT10D power plants were also studied. In the true MDC tradition of frugality, some trade studies included many DC-10 components, and this concept rapidly became the primary focus, leading to a rather stubby looking aircraft. The final design selected was designated D-969N-21, offered to the airlines in July 1978.

It featured an all-new, super-critical wing and retained the DC-10's cockpit, forward fuselage, rear cabin section plus a modified over-wing cabin section. The DC-10's overall fuselage length was reduced by 30 feet, 2 inches in the new model, now named DC-X-200 for sales brochure purposes. Having dispensed with the center engine, an all-new empennage was introduced. Though similar to the DC-10 Twin design, the horizontal stabilizers were reduced from the 71-foot, 2-inch span to just 50 feet, 11 inches. The redesigned vertical stabilizer brought the DC-X-200's overall height down to 50 feet. The new 153-foot, 8-inch-long wing incorporated variable camber Krueger flaps on the leading edges and two-segment linkage flaps. The proposed power plants were GE CF6-45s rated at 45,000 pounds of thrust.

Maximum takeoff weight was 293,000 pounds with a MLW of 260,000 pounds. Fuel capacity was 83,200 pounds with a payload of 74,750 pounds. The primary seating arrangement was 20 in six-across first-class (2-2-2) at a 38-inch pitch, plus 210 economy-class in nine-abreast seating (2-5-2) at a 34-inch pitch. The forward belly could carry eight LD-3 pallets plus 10 more in the rear compartment. Both compartments featured 70-inch by 66-inch doors with an optional 104-inch by 66-inch aft door available. The aft bulk-cargo compartment in the tail – normally used for last-minute baggage - had 510 cubic feet of space available.

As part of the new technology approach, liberal use of composite material was incorporated into the design. Including were cabin floor beams and struts, cargo floor beams, control surfaces, wing fixed trailing edge and wing-body and tail fairings. A digital flight guidance and control system was introduced. Even with these improvements, about 90 percent of rotable units retained commonality with the DC-10-30 and 85 percent were common to the Series 10.

While these studies were being developed, MDC entered into an informal agreement with the French manufacturer Marcel Dassault to work on the design of a new Advanced Short Medium Range (ASMR) aircraft. The intent was to use the fuselage of the Dassault Mercure, of which only 10 were ever sold, and marry a stretched version to the supercritical wing being developed by MDC. Versions of the A-300 with the super-critical wing were also examined for a brief period. However, this alliance did not last long.

Unfortunately, the DC-X-200 found little favor with the airlines and the proposal was dropped by the end of 1978.

---

when demand returned following the expected economic recovery. The strategy paid off when KLM ordered a third Series 30 for Philippine Airlines on November 26.

On the same day, Thai International also purchased two Series 30s plus one option to replace the leased aircraft. Iberia negotiated for two more with its latest additions being capable of carrying the spare engine pod. Malaysian bought three more, Garuda purchased two and Swissair picked up one additional aircraft, bringing the total to 11 new firm orders. Some contracts were not made public until early 1976. In spite of the price break, none of the U.S. airlines expressed interest in additional aircraft. The order book showed that 228 firm plus 30 options had been received with 210 delivered by December 31. Forty-three DC-10s were delivered in 1975, but the rate would then drop to one per month.

The year closed with a statement released by MDC in connection with the previously mentioned SEC hearings. The company admitted that, like Lockheed, Northrop, Exxon, Boeing and others, it had made payments to overseas agents in some countries for distribution to government and airline officials. In its statement, the company disclosed payments totaling $2.5 million – some of it questionable – had been paid between 1970 and 1975.

JAL Buildup

Following two unrelated accidents in November and December, ONA ordered two new DC-10-30CFs on April 22, 1976, for spring 1977 delivery. A third was scheduled for delivery in October 1977. Western also added another Series 10 on May 5.

The first of four closely spaced deliveries was made to Japan Air Lines on April 9. The airline initiated domestic services on July 1 between Tokyo and Sapporo three times a day plus a daily service between Tokyo and Fukuoka.

At the delivery ceremony for its seventh DC-10 on June 9, Air New Zealand's general manager stated that the company had just ordered an additional aircraft and, in the United Kingdom, British Caledonian signed for two DC-10-30s and two options. Air Afrique ordered a third Series 30 on July 6 for spring 1979 delivery. Lufthansa contracted for a ninth aircraft in September, and Thai picked up two more Series 30s during November.

The Gamble Pays Off

The decision to keep the production line open while losing money paid off as a recovery cycle in airline traffic began to emerge. On January 20, 1977, American's board approved the purchase of three additional DC-10s. Nigeria Airways added a second aircraft on March 4, and Wardair Canada became a DC-10 customer on March 8 with an order for two Series 30s equipped with a 301-seat tourist-class layout. The surge continued with World Airways taking three Series 30CFs plus three options on March 22. In contrast, World's charter layout was for 380 seats in a 10-abreast configuration. Meanwhile, British Caledonian's first DC-10 was delivered on March 18 and entered service two days later on West African routes. JAL added a seventh and eighth aircraft on May 6, both for late 1978 delivery. These new orders led MDC to increase the production rate from one to 2.1 per month by January 1978.

Garuda DC-10-30 PK-GIF (ln 286/msn 46686) on a test flight in August 1979. Below, the airline joined the "all-white" club in the 1990s. PK-GIA (ln 223/msn 46918) appears below on finals at Hong Kong's Kai Tak Airport in November 1993.

Nigerian Airways DC-10-30 5N-ANN (ln 231/msn 46957) in delivery markings.

Author

World Airways revised its DC-10 color schemes frequently. N109WA (ln 314/msn 47819) wears the delivery scheme. Below, N112WA (ln 317/msn 47820) was photographed in 1987. Bottom, DC-10-10 N1827U (ln 198/msn 46626) poses at Los Angeles in 1986.

Author's Collection

Jukka Kauppinen

JAT's first DC-10-30 (YU-AMA, In 259/msn 46981) was repossessed in 1992 and leased to Air Liberte. (Author's Collection)

After being stored during the 1992-96 war in Yugoslavia, YU-AMB (In 278/msn 46988) emerged in new colors. The aircraft appears with enlarged titles. (Author's Collection)

Continental introduced nine-abreast DC-10 seating for its 1977 summer services to Hawaii. Six aircraft were modified with new center seat units that could be converted to either four or five seats by using different arm-rest combinations; this increased the coach-class capacity to 218. By the end of 1977, Continental had removed all pub lounges from its fleet and installed higher-density seating, thus adding the equivalent of four DC-10s to its fleet. American also began testing the layout in some markets.

Composite Testing

As part of its Aircraft Energy Efficiency program, NASA awarded MDC a $15.6 million contract on May 13 to develop and evaluate composite vertical stabilizers for the DC-10. MDC agreed to contribute an additional $1.7 million to the effort. The contract was for six and one-half years. A composite fin box was flight-tested on a KC-10 in 1983. It weighed 23 percent less than the metal structure. Upper sections of the rudder made from carbon fiber-reinforced plastic were fitted to 13 DC-10s operated by six airlines worldwide. Much of the gained experience was incorporated into the C-17 military transport, which embodies many composite structural components.

DC-10 orders continued to come in, with Martinair adding a fourth Series 30CF on June 7 and VIASA taking three Series 30s on July 11; both orders were for 1978 delivery. Singapore Airlines joined the ranks of DC-10-30 customers on July 12, ordering four after a fierce competition with Boeing.

In June, to the consternation of MDC salesmen who had campaigned vigorously, an article in Aviation Week & Space Technology announced that Yugoslav Air Transport (JAT) intended to order Boeing 747SPs. John Wallace – famous for the "hams for DC-9s" deal with the Yugoslavs – and R.E.G. Davies, manager of market research, quickly headed for Belgrade to do some serious legwork. Their efforts were successful and, on July 18, JAT signed a contract for two DC-10-30s. Another order for three DC-10s came from American on August 1, increasing its fleet to 31. Swissair charter subsidiary Balair became the 42nd DC-10 customer when it ordered a Series 30 on September 19.

Skytrain Launch

At the beginning of October, Laker brought its Series 10 total to six by adding two for 1979 delivery. The airline had launched the Skytrain low-fare scheduled service between Gatwick and New York on September 26. Initially, Laker could not sell seats on the flight until 4 a.m. on the day of travel, but this rule was later rescinded.

British Caledonian increased its order to four Series 30s by exercising options on October 13, and CP Air finally joined the customer ranks on October 14, ordering two Series 30s plus two options. Later, UTA, which had given up an earlier position for Martinair, added one more order in December.

The year-end commercial sales total had increased to 275 firm plus 30 conditional orders and options. Two hundred forty-five had been delivered to 35 airlines.

Singapore Airlines bought seven DC-10-30s, including 9V-SDA (ln 260/msn 46990), which was sold to Wardair three years later.

Delivered in January 1985, Finnair DC-10-30 OH-LHA (ln 181/msn 47956) was long-term leased to Air Liberte.

Balair DC-10-30 HB-IHK (ln 267/msn 46998) differed from Swissair's DC-10s only in the seating plan.

Built for ONA, DC-10-30 N1035F (In 257/msn 46992) was instead leased by Icelandic in the winter of 1979-80 from Seaboard World, which bought but never operated it. (Author's Collection)

CP Air DC-10-30 C-GCPE (In 295/msn 46542) reflects its delivery colors (above) and later Canadian markings (below).

British operator Airtours acquired DC-10-30 OY-CNO (ln 260/msn 46990) when it bought Premiair in 1996. (Author's Collection)

As a short-lived subsidiary, Aloha Pacific operated Series 30 N801AL (ln 159/msn 46933) in 1984. (Author's Collection)

AVCOM was the first Russian DC-10 operator. An ex-Martinair Series 30CF, it was registered UN10200 (ln 127/msn 46891) in 1994 then changed to RA100200. (via Eddy Gual)

A new DC-10 operator in 1999, Avensa leased an ex-VARIG Series 30 PP-VMB as YV-50C (ln 156/msn 46945). (Andrea Ponteralo)

DC-10-30 OO-JOT (ln 63/msn 46850) in Challenge Air Cargo colors and, below, on a sublease to Corsair in 1997. It was originally built for UTA.

Paul Bannwarth

Avimage

U.K.-based DAS Air Cargo carries flowers for Tele Flower Auctions, hence the TFA titles on the engine of DC-10-30F N400JR (In 254/msn 46976). (Cristofer Witt)

Eastern leased three ex-Alitalia DC-10-30s beginning in 1985, including N391EA (In 149/msn 47866), later acquired by Continental as N13067. (Author's Collection)

Series 30 F-OKBB (In 259/msn 46981) operated by ExpressOne on charters in 1993-94. (Malcolm Nason)

Gemini Air Cargo's DC-10-30F N601GC (ln 117/msn 47921) in original colors was converted for all-freight use in 1995. Below, N606GC (ln 196/msn 47929) wears revised 1996 markings. Both are ex-Lufthansa.

The breakup of Aeroflot led to many new companies, including Krasnoyarskavia (KRASAir) which leased two ex KLM DC-10-30s N525MD (ln 46/msn 46550) and N533MD (ln 82/msn 46553, shown) from MDC for three years beginning in 1993. (Author's Collection)

Replacing aircraft lost in the Gulf War of 1991, Kuwait Airways leased BA DC-10-30 G-NIUK (ln 158/msn 46932). (Mike Axe)

ILFC bought ANZ DC-10-30 ZK-NZR (ln 213/msn 47849) in 1982, then leased it to Linhas Aereas de Mozambique as F-GDJK. It later migrated to AOM. (Author's Collection)

LAN-Chile leased DC-10-30 CC-CJT (ln 242/msn 46950) from Air New Zealand during 1982-86. It was sold to American Airlines as N164AA. (Airline Photos)

Named after famous Canadian bush pilot Wop May, Wardair DC-10-30 C-GXRC (In 256/msn 46978) was sold to GPA in 1988.

The year 1978 began well with JAL adding a fifth Series 40 order on January 27. Wardair increased its fleet to four with two Series 30s on March 10. A few days later, World Airways and CP Air exercised options for three Series 30CFs and two Series 30s respectively. Then Western ordered two more Series 10s and reserved options for four more, followed on April 28 by United's purchase of five Series 10s, bringing its fleet to 42; the airline also added 10 options.

Strike

A major shop worker's union, the United Automobile Workers (UAW), went on strike in January after rejecting a new contract offer from the company. It lasted three months but, ironically, the unions eventually settled for the original offer. In the interim, MDC drafted many white collar workers to the shop floor in an effort to keep the production lines open. Several aircraft were completed and delivered during the strike. Fortunately, the impact on the customer airlines was not great, due to either low seasonal traffic demand or coincidental fiscal concerns.

Continued Sales Success

As the production line recovered its tempo, sales continued, starting with a new order from Condor on June 16 for two Series 30s plus an option; Swissair added two more on July 7, bringing its fleet to 11 Series 30s. This order brought the firm sales total to 300 aircraft. A few days later, the Japanese cabinet announced that three DC-10s would be purchased for a VIP fleet and operated by the Japanese Air Self Defense Force, but the order was never consummated. A new government, under Prime Minister Ohira,

Condor DC-10-30 D-ADQO (In 301/msn 46596) reflects the original bare-metal scheme, disliked by assemblers as it required special skin panel handling.

Ariana's DC-10-30 YA-LAS (ln 291/msn 47888) on a test flight with a protective film still covering the polished-metal skin.

dropped the requirement as part of an economy drive in January 1979. Ariana Afghan signed a Letter of Intent for one DC-10-30 plus an option on July 24, although the final contract wasn't completed until January 3, 1979. Singapore Airlines picked up the first of its options on August 8, and British Caledonian signed for three more Series 30s on August 14.

Laker Does A Deal

Not to be outdone by his neighbor and competitor British Caledonian, Freddie Laker announced the purchase of five DC-10-30s on September 19. Laker was the first to buy a model with a 580,000-pound MTOW, made possible by the introduction of GE CF6-50C2B engines rated at 54,000 pounds of thrust. Then operating Series 10 services to Los Angeles with a fuel stop in Bangor, Maine, Laker needed nonstop capability to remain competitive. He also had ideas of operating round-the-world services for $999. Part of the package included upgrading the Series 10s in his fleet. Under some weather conditions, some Series 10 flights to the United States and Canada were forced to make unscheduled fuel stops. MDC agreed to install an additional fuel cell in the center section and add structural reinforcement to raise the MTOW by 15,000 pounds to 455,000 pounds.

Back to Normal

On September 28, Singapore Airlines converted two more options to firm, just prior to taking delivery of its first delayed aircraft. The airline actually inaugurated DC-10 service with an aircraft leased from Martinair on October 1. JAL ordered another five Series 40s on October 9, four for international services and one for domestic operations. A new order for three more Series 30CFs and three options was received from World Airways on October 18 for spring 1980 delivery.

JAT's first DC-10 was delivered in December, flying 6,300 miles nonstop from Long Beach to Belgrade in 11 hours, 20 minutes.

Continental Goes Intercontinental

Continental ordered its first two Series 30s, plus two options, on February 8, 1979, just a day after Western had exercised two more Series 10 options. Continental's new aircraft were for its Pacific route expansion. The airline decided to re-introduce a first-class lounge on these aircraft. The aircraft seating layout was for 22 first-class and 223 coach-class passengers. On domestic sectors, the lounge area quickly converted to 22 additional Coach class seats. American confirmed an order for one Series 30 on February 2.

At the end of March, total sales stood at 330 firm plus conditional firm and options for 50 more; 273 DC-10s had been delivered. Among the deliveries was the first Series 30 for CP Air on March 29. This aircraft had previously been intended for National and was partially painted when offered to CP Air for early delivery. National had run into financial trouble and was looking for a merger partner. New orders continued as Laker added one more aircraft on March 21, and Philippine Airlines contracted for a Series 30, its fourth, plus two options on March 30. Air Afrique signed for its third Series 30 on April 4.

World Airways emulated Laker Airways on April 11 when it introduced a $99.99 fare between the U.S. West Coast and Newark and Baltimore. Tickets could be purchased in advance through a major ticketing outlet, Ticketron. As with Laker, meal tickets were sold separately.

The Brazilian government authorized VARIG to buy six DC-10-30s on May 2 for delivery in 1980-81, but only five were ordered and delivered. The U.S. Export-Import Bank announced approval of a loan to Egyptair for the purchase of four DC-10-30s on May 8, although MDC never announced this order because Egyptair did not have its government's formal consent.

A rush of orders were announced on May 10 when United converted five options to firm buys, bringing the total to 47, and Alitalia ordered six more Series 30s for 1981-82 delivery. This order included two Series 30AFs – the first to be ordered – and one DC-10-30CF. JAL also added four 277-seat intercontinental Series 40s and one 370-seat single-class model for domestic services, bringing the fleet total to 14. A week later, Iberia signed for a ninth plus two options.

On May 21, Mexicana chose a DC-10-10 powered by the GE CF6-45B2, a CF6-50C2 derated to 46,500 pounds of thrust. The variant was designed to handle Mexico City's high altitude and ambient temperatures. At the time of the announcement, no specific numbers of aircraft were announced. Two days later, SABENA received government approval to purchase a fourth Series 30CF.

The Chicago Disaster

An American Airlines DC-10 crashed immediately after taking off from Chicago's O'Hare International Airport on May 25, 1979, when the left engine and pylon separated during rotation. All 271 people on board plus two on the ground were killed when the aircraft impacted in a full left bank attitude from an altitude of 325 feet. The official cause was found to be "an asymmetrical stall and ensuing roll because of uncommanded retraction of the left wing outboard leading-edge slats, and loss of stall

To expand Skytrain service, Laker bought six Series 30s. G-BGXE (ln 302/msn 47811) was sold to United as N1853U after Laker's demise. (Bruce Drum)

In 1996, Laker started a new airline in the United States with three DC-10-30s including N831LA (ln 147/msn 46936). (George Ditchfield)

Partially painted when National merged with Pan Am, DC-10-30 N88NA (ln 268/msn 46540) was resold to CP Air as C-GCPC, leading to this unusual livery. It used an MDC test registration (N8715Q) before delivery and never flew as N88NA. (Tim Williams)

Wearing test registration N19B, Mexicana DC-10-15 (ln 346/msn 48258) became N1003L in service.

In the early 1990s, Mexicana revamped its livery as reflected by DC-10-15 N10045 (ln 357/msn 48259), photographed at JFK. (A. J. Smith)

warning and slat disagreement indication systems resulting from maintenance-induced damage leading to the separation of the No. 1 engine and pylon assembly at a critical point during takeoff. The separation resulted from damage by improper maintenance procedures which led to failure of the pylon structure."

When the engine-pylon combination departed, it broke upwards, tearing off part of the leading edge and damaging the hydraulic jack which actuated the left wing leading-edge slats. This allowed the slats to retract under aerodynamic pressure. The pilots could not see that the engine had departed due to the forward location of the cockpit. The slat retraction caused the left wing to stall since the aircraft – in a 14-degree nose up attitude – was below minimum speed for operating with closed slats; this induced the fatal roll. At the same time, electrical failure caused by loss of the No. 1 engine-mounted generators resulted in the loss of vital stall-warning cockpit instrumentation. Interestingly, MDC had installed dual stall-warning systems in the DC-10, but in 1971, some U.S. airlines including American, received FAA authority to operate with a single system. The FAA withdrew that approval following the accident.

The FAA's Reaction

Upon finding of a broken three-inch diameter forward thrust link attachment bolt on the departure runway, the FAA issued an Airworthiness Directive (AD) on May 28, requiring all DC-10 operators to inspect all four bolts which took the loads created by the engine's thrust. Other fasteners held the pylon to the wing. Many airlines chose to replace all four bolts, a simple procedure that did not require the removal of the engine or pylon. After inspection, many DC-10s began flying again. But an amended AD to inspect the pylon structure was triggered on May 29 when a United mechanic found severe damage to a pylon bulkhead web. As the fleet was re-checked, four other American and two Continental DC-10-10s were found to have cracked upper flanges on the forward bulkhead of the pylon. It was also learned that two Continental DC-10s had cracked flanges repaired in earlier instances after engine-pylon removals. So, on May 30, FAA Administrator Langhorne Bond grounded all FAA-registered DC-10s. Foreign aviation authorities followed suit, grounding the DC-10 fleet worldwide. At the time, 275 were in service, so the action had an enormous impact on air travel.

The FAA withdrew the Airworthiness Certificate of all American-registered aircraft on June 6 and, on June 26, banned all DC-10s from U.S. air space. However, no damage was found on any Series 30s or any foreign-registered Series 10s and, by June 30, these aircraft were flying again everywhere except to the United States. Strong protests from foreign airlines, particularly European carriers, were to no avail. Freddie Laker threatened legal action against the U.S. authorities for refusing to allow his U.K.-certificated aircraft to enter the United States. He got around part of the ban by flying U.S.-bound passengers to Windsor, Ontario and busing the passengers across the border to Detroit. Several other major European airlines banded together to sue the FAA on similar grounds in November, citing the Chicago Convention of 1944, an international treaty which states that "all parties recognize the airworthiness certificates of all the other parties."

American's Series 10 N134AA (ln 321/msn 47829) reflects "American Airlines LuxuryLiner" titles on the nose. (A. J. Smith)

The Cause

Because the damaged aircraft appeared to be confined to just three U.S. Series 10 operators, attention soon focused on their methods of removing the engine and pylon. An MDC Service Bulletin required that three spherical bearings mounted on the two pylon bulkheads be replaced at certain intervals during engine removal. MDC's maintenance manuals suggested that the engine be removed before the pylon was detached from the wing, which took about 200 man hours. However, neither the FAA nor the manufacturer had the legal authority to approve or disapprove customer maintenance procedures, and the three airlines in question had devised procedures to remove the engine and pylon as a combined unit. United elected to use an overhead crane but Continental and American engineers developed a method of supporting the engine and pylon with a large forklift while removing the combined unit from the wing. American also reversed the sequence of removing the bearing bolts and bushings that attached the forward bulkhead assembly. The airline had previously tried this while working on four Series 30s owned by a foreign airline; inspection after re-installment had revealed no sign of damage. Unfortunately, the design clearances of the Series 30 bulkhead installation were greater than those of the Series 10 and the heavier engine, supported by stronger structure, was more damage tolerant. The inability to control the forklift movements to tighter limits with its approximately 18,000-pound load led to damage being caused during the removal of the unit. At the time of the American crash, the aircraft had flown 341 hours since the last "C" check when the engine had been removed.

American Airlines was subsequently fined $500,000, and Continental $100,000 for violating FAA-approved DC-10 maintenance procedures.

On July 13, 1979, the FAA restored the DC-10's Type Certificate (No. AW22E) to the relief of DC-10 operators worldwide. In spite of dire predictions, re-introduction of the DC-10 encountered no resistance from the foreign flying public and load factors quickly resumed their normal levels. Some U.S. domestic airlines were slower to overcome the resistance, but by October load factors began returning to normal.

Fortunately, the flight data and cockpit voice recorders were recovered, so it was possible to re-create the crew's actions. A flight simulator was programmed to recreate the loss of an engine and its associated systems, along with the dissimilar slat settings. Thirteen pilots then completed 70 takeoffs using the same flight profile. In the tests, all the pilots who followed the flight director indications crashed. But some pilots who were aware of the doomed aircraft's flight profile and recognized the situation, pushed the nose down, increased power and flew out of the problem to land safely.

In addition to these tests, MDC instrumented a Series 10 and Series 30, then carried out test flights to confirm the loads on the pylon. At Langley, Virginia, the National Aeronautics and Space Administration (NASA)

carried out wind tunnel tests of a model with simulated leading-edge damage and the engine removed. Various dissimilar slat extensions were then tested. New fatigue tests were made on a pylon assembly and all the previous calculations revisited by MDC engineers and the FAA.

MDC did revise the design to improve the clearances, but the change was only required on 15 aircraft. Most airlines switched to the MDC pylon-wing interface inspection schedule to prevent future incidents.

Canceled Orders

On June 15, Alitalia's Board of Directors refused to confirm the recent order for six DC-10s, eliminating production of the DC-10AF. American subsequently let three options drop as their decision date passed. Egyptair canceled its order in August when the Egyptian government refused payment authorization. However, this setback was due entirely to fiscal considerations.

On the plus side, CP Air purchased four Series 30s in June, and Continental bought one on August 2, for its proposed services to China. AeroMexico confirmed an order for two DC-10-15s on September 9. This was the identical model selected by Mexicana, but the first time the new designation was announced. Mexicana formally signed for two Series 15s on September 26, becoming the 46th customer. JAL added three more Series 40s on October 10. SABENA placed another Series 30CF order on November 5, and Malaysian added a third Series 30 on November 29.

Legal Problems

Based on a suit filed by Pakistan International Airlines, two members of MDC's board plus two other employees were indicted by a Federal Grand Jury on November 9, charged with illegal payments in connection with the sale of aircraft overseas. Nine months later, the U.S. Department of Justice also filed a civil suit against the company and the four accused, to recover part of the funding which had been obtained from the Export-Import Bank to fund the purchase of PIA's DC-10s. As mentioned earlier, other major corporations had received similar charges. Eventually, in September 1981, the parties pleaded guilty to PIA's civil suit and criminal charges after initially pleading not guilty because the previous Pakistani government was aware of the payoffs. MDC paid a fine of $1.2 million but charges against the four officials were dropped.

Stretch Refinements

By September 1979, continued trade-off studies had modified the stretch DC-10 design in a number of ways. A long-range version dubbed DC-10-62 featured a fuselage with a 100-inch plug ahead of the wings and retained the 220-inch rear plug. The tail cone had been extended by 40 inches to reduce drag in line with the latest changes to the DC-10. New active ailerons reduced wing bending moments, allowing an increased

Artist's impression of the DC-10-62 over Manhattan.

wing span of 175 feet, 4 inches. To eliminate the nose-up flying attitude, the wing box was rotated two degrees nose-up, providing a level floor and improved performance in cruise. But the biggest change was to the flap system. Its small, vaned version of the standard DC-10 was replaced by a double-hinged flap that increased the chord during takeoff and landing. Fitted with GE CF6-50C1 or P&W JT9D-7R4H engines rated at 56,000 pounds thrust, takeoff distances were reduced by 800 feet and larger ground spoilers helped reduce landing distances. The MTOW had increased to 620,000 pounds with a Maximum Landing Weight of 446,000 pounds. With an overall length of 206 feet, 11 inches, the Series 62 could carry 353 passengers (versus 275 in the standard DC-10) in a mixed-class layout over 5,500 miles.

Two variants of the 40-foot stretched Series 61 for the domestic and Series 63 for the intercontinental versions were also updated. Both could carry 393 mixed-class passengers in an upper galley configuration. The Series 61 utilized the existing wing of the Series 30/40 with the increased angle of incidence and called for GE CF6-50C2 engines derated to 46,500 pounds of thrust with an MTOW of 520,000 pounds. The Series 63, which combined the fuselage of the Series 61 and the wing, engines and associated weights of the Series 62, had a range of more than 4,800 miles. Another proposal, the DC-10 VLR (Very Long-Range) incorporated a DC-10 fuselage with the Series 62 wing, engines and MTOW, creating a range of 6,600 miles.

Two More Accidents

The DC-10's bad luck continued when unrelated accidents destroyed two aircraft within a month. On October 31, a Western DC-10-10 landed on a closed runway in poor visibility at Mexico City, struck a heavy construction vehicle during an attempted go-around and crashed into a building. Then an Air New Zealand DC-10-30 on a sight-seeing flight to Antarctica collided with Mt. Erebus in white-out conditions on November 28. The cause was attributed to pilot error because the DC-10 was below the preplanned

altitude at the time of impact. However, it was later revealed that a navigational error had been entered into the computerized flight plan and ANZ's management was later accused of trying to conceal the fact.

Both accidents resulted in heavy loss of life, but the DC-10 and its systems were exonerated of any responsibility. Even so, the media in general continued to give the aircraft a bad name, using words like "jinxed" in their rush to grab attention. MDC put a great deal of effort into countering this misinformation, but it appeared to have little effect. The December 21 issue of National Transportation Safety Board's (NTSB) Accident Report NTSB-AAR-79-17 covering the Chicago crash was too late to save the DC-10's reputation. The FAA accident findings were similar to the NTSB report, although some minor changes were required for the pylons on the 113 Series 10s then in service. However, the FAA received negative comments for its initial handling of the situation and the unnecessary DC-10 grounding.

In spite of the strike and the three accidents, 36 DC-10s were delivered in 1979 with 34 new orders received. The total order book stood at 352 firm plus 38 options; 299 aircraft had been delivered. At the end of 1979, after an intensive sales effort directed particularly at Air New Zealand, United, Swissair and Lufthansa, work on stretched versions was put on hold. None of the airlines foresaw a need for the type in the near term, so the planned first deliveries were rescheduled for mid-1984.

Major Merger and New Operators

The merger of Pan American World Airways and National Airlines on January 16, 1980, led to Pan Am taking delivery of the last DC-10 previously ordered by National, adding yet another customer to the list. Mexicana contracted for a third Series 15 on February 14, retaining two further options. Repeat orders came for one Series 30, its eighth, from British Caledonian on March 11 and two plus two options from CP Air on March 13; all three firm orders were for 1981 delivery.

In January 1990, Pan Am acquired National's fleet through a merger. DC-10-30 N80NA (ln 105/msn 46711) was later sold to American and destroyed in 1993. (Author's Collection)

A minor aviation historical point was achieved on March 7, when a JAL DC-10 became the first widebody jetliner to initiate service to the People's Republic of China.

The Federal Express Corporation (FedEx) took delivery of the first of four DC-10-10CFs from Continental on March 19 with an option for the remaining four. Negotiations had started in February 1979, but were not resolved until October. The five-year old aircraft were sold for approximately $24 million each. After a few minor modifications to convert from a pallet system to containers, the first revenue service was flown from Los Angeles to Memphis, Tennessee on March 24. Regular service between Memphis and Newark was initiated on March 31. FedEx eventually incorporated a number of enhancements on its DC-10 fleet, including increasing the MTOW by 7,500 pounds.

Asian Problems

MDC salesmen began encountering difficulty in selling DC-10s to Asian airlines in early 1980. Initially, it was believed that the Chicago accident was a major factor; however, the real reason turned out to be the rapid growth in the Pacific and Asian markets and frequency limits on intercontinental routes from Asia to Europe and the United States. Singapore Airlines decided to standardize on the Boeing 747, quickly followed by Malaysian and Thai International. Increasing numbers of A-300s were carrying regional traffic, so the DC-10s were squeezed out. The decision not to build the stretched DC-10s was beginning to tell. It was a difficult choice but, except for Pacific and Asia, airline traffic generally had begun yet another cyclical downturn. In the previous six months, the world's airlines had reported combined losses of more than $500 million. At the end of the fiscal year in March, MDC had received orders for just 26 new DC-10s versus 42 in the previous year. Due to the slower sales, the decision was made to reduce the production rate to two per month by June 1981.

Extended Range

Swissair ordered two DC-10-30ERs on July 9. The engines were upgraded to CF6-50C2Bs rated at 54,000 pounds of thrust to allow the MTOW to increase to 557,500 pounds. A 1,530-gallon auxiliary fuel tank was installed in the rear of the lower aft cargo compartment, increasing the range by 700 miles. These changes were to allow Swissair to operate the DC-10 nonstop from Switzerland to Rio de Janeiro. A contract to upgrade two of the existing fleet was also signed.

July also saw the launch of a massive MDC publicity campaign, headed by former astronaut Charles "Pete" Conrad, then vice president of marketing at Long Beach. This was in response to requests by some airlines that were still suffering the aftermath of the three 1979 accidents.

Mexicana ordered two more Series 15s on July 11, bringing the total to five. The engines, although the same as mentioned earlier, were re-designated CF6-50C2-F. The biggest foreign operator of DC-10s, JAL placed an order for its 18th and 19th Series 40s on August 18 for late 1981 and early 1982 delivery.

A New Chairman

James S. McDonnell, Chairman of MDC and the man responsible for the DC-10's existence, passed away on August 22, 1980. He founded the original McDonnell Aircraft Corporation on July 6, 1939, and became chairman of MDC after the merger with Douglas Aircraft Company on April 26, 1967. His nephew, Sanford N. McDonnell, who became much more involved in the commercial sales side of the business, replaced Old Mac.

CRAF

For six years, the U.S. Air Force had been trying to persuade U.S. airlines to buy widebody jets modified to meet a military requirement in times of national emergency. Aircraft in this program would be part of the Civil Reserve Air Fleet (CRAF). Generally, this entailed a strengthened floor and large cargo door. The Air Force would be willing to pay for the upgrade and some additional funding towards the higher operating costs, but most airlines declined the offer, as the funding did not offset the loss in payload range. However, in August 1980, United finally accepted a contract whereby the military would reimburse the airline $17.4 million, of which $9 million went towards the purchase of a single DC-10-30CF for delivery in May 1982. Part of this was to offset the cost of delayed delivery for conversion of a new aircraft, as the tooling was not available at the time.

On October 26, Continental put its first Series 30s into service on the Los Angeles–Aukland–Sydney route. The year ended with orders from CP Air for a seventh DC-10 on December 22, while Laker bought another Series 30 on December 29 and Ghana Airways ordered its first Series 30 on December 31.

Author's Collection

United acquired a number of used Series 30s in the early 1980s: N1854U (ln 312/msn 47813), above, and N1853U (ln 303/msn 47812), below, were both formerly with Laker and converted to freighters. Bottom, N1855U (ln 328/msn 47837) is ex-Pan Am.

Roy Lock

Author's Collection

Owned by GPA, DC-10-30 N602DC (ln 254/msn 46976) was leased to Lineas Aereas Paraguayas in 1992 and subsequently replaced by VARIG Series 30 PP-VMX (ln 356/msn 47845), shown below with modified titles.

LOT-Polish Airlines operated two DC-10-30s between 1993 and 1995, including 9M-MAT (ln 240/msn 46640) from Malaysian. (via Eddy Gual)

DC-10-30 F-GKMY (ln 325/msn 47815) of Minerve, which became part of AOM in 1992. (via Eddy Gual)

Corporate-owned, Minebea's DC-10-30CF N10MB (ln 157/msn 47907) was acquired from SABENA in 1994. (Author's Collection)

First sold to Zambia, U.K. charter airline Monarch began operating DC-10-30 G-DMCA (ln 348/msn 48266) in 1996. (via Eddy Gual)

Uruguay flag carrier PLUNA leased a single DC-10-30 PP-VMW (ln 336/msn 47844) leased from VARIG. (Martin Stamm)

Zaire carrier Scribe Air leased DC-10-30 F-GHOI (ln 217/msn 46870) in 1994 for one year. (Author's Collection)

Skyjet Brazil operated several DC-10s in Latin America. The only Series 30 was PP-AJM (ln 196/msn 47929). (Author's Collection)

Destroyed at Malaga in September 1982, Spantax DC-10-30CF EC-DEG (ln 238/msn 46962) wears the airline's 1950s livery. Below, Series 30 EC-DUG (ln 73/msn 46576) shows the revised colors of 1984. (both Author's Collection)

Argentine carrier STAF Cargo leased DC-10-30F XA-TDC (ln 127/msn 46891) from TAESA. Earlier, it served with Martinair, AvCom and Malaysian. (via Eddy Gual)

Aptly named, Transaero DC-10-30 N140AA (ln 106/msn 46712) poses at LAX in July 1998. (Michael Carter/Aero Pacific Images)

Transair International's DC-10-15 PP-OOO (ln 346/msn 48258) previously served with Mexicana and AeroPeru. Below, the same aircraft, wearing N1003L, was intended for World Brazilian Air in 1997, but the deal never came to fruition.

Ecuatoriana leased ex-Swissair DC-10-30 HC-BKO (ln 57/msn 46575) beginning in 1983. Stored, it re-entered service in 1996 wearing VASP colors and Ecuatoriana titles.

Appropriately registered G-LYON (ln 305/msn 47818), Caledonian Series 30 was leased from Boeing. (Avimage)

VASP leased DC-10-30 PP-SON (ln 200/msn 47868) for one year in 1991. Below, cargo operations are flown by VASPEX using DC-10-30 N107WA (ln 280/msn 46836) on lease from World Airways. (both via Eddy Gual)

Hawaiian leased two additional DC-10-30s at the end of 1999 for use on charter flights to Tahiti. Shown is ex-Continental N68060 (ln 331/msn 47850) with special titles recognizing the carrier's 70th anniversary. (Michael Corlett)

Chapter XIII

MILITARY VERSIONS

Ship One assumes the receiver position below Ship Eight during initial flight trials.

For some time, the U.S. Air Force had been seeking a larger aircraft to supplement its KC-135 tanker fleet. A series of dummy air-to-air refueling trials were flown near Edwards AFB late in March 1972, using two DC-10s to determine if the center engine exhaust plume or any other wake problems would create stability problems for a large receiving aircraft. Earlier, Boeing initiated a similar series of tests using the prototype 747.

Meanwhile, in response to a Long Range Patrol Aircraft (LRPA) requirement issued by the Canadian Armed Forces in late 1972, designs were created to offer suitable versions of both the DC-10-10CF and the DC-10 Twin. In a substantial offset program, MDC offered to have bare aircraft delivered to Malton for fitting out by its Canadian employees. The DC-10 LRPA design, based on the Series 10CF, put the tactical crew with its sensor-electronic systems in a closed compartment behind the cockpit. The remainder of the main deck could accommodate cargo or 204 troops. The rear section became a crew rest area and sonobuoy storage and launch area. The lower galley area was replaced by observation stations and avionics racks. The forward cargo hold was retained while the rear compartment held additional fuel tanks and a weapons bay. Wingtip mounted in-flight refueling pods and under-wing weapons stations were also proposed. However, the Canadians eventually elected to purchase cheaper, customized versions of the Lockheed P-3A Orion turboprop for the mission.

The Tanker Takes Shape

What would become known as the KC-10 began with initial DC-10 tanker studies for the Strategic Air Command, with removable bladder tanks and pumps located on the main deck and the belly available for cargo. Based on the Series 30CF, these studies increased the MTOW to 605,000 pounds utilizing GE's 52,500-pound-thrust F103-GE-100 (later designated CF6-50C1) or the P&W JT9D-59A. A revised proposal, dubbed Advanced Tanker/Cargo Aircraft (ATCA) began to gel in March 1974. The MTOW was eventually reduced to 590,000 pounds with only minor structural and landing gear changes to accommodate heavier loads. The increased takeoff maneuver loads could be handled by restricting the aircraft to 2.3g compared with 2.5g on commercial DC-10 flights.

The engine choice was GE's CF6-50C2. The extra fuel tanks were relocated to the lower cargo compartments. The forward tanks held 53,655 pounds and the aft tanks 64,174 pounds of fuel. The twin-keel members and additional crushable material beneath the tanks added safety in the event of a wheels-up landing. The 238,236 pounds of fuel in the aircraft's own tanks were also transferable. A total fuel capacity of 356,065 pounds of JP-4 allowed the tanker to fly 1,000 miles, off-load 255,000 pounds of fuel to receiving aircraft and return to base with standard fuel reserves. Fuel could be dispensed via a boom to almost every aircraft in the U.S. Air Force inventory, controlled from a new "boomer" position in the rear ventral position. The boom and fuel transfer system, designed and developed by MDC, was unique in that fuel could be

Model of the proposed modified DC-10 to meet the Canadian LRPA requirement. (Courtesy of Tony Paradiso)

The 15th Air Force KC-10, AF79-1951 (ln 380/msn 48211) from March AFB, refuels a B-2 bomber over the California desert.

transferred in either direction. The boom tip also incorporated a device that could lock onto the receiver aircraft's refueling receptacle and essentially drag the aircraft. It was developed after numerous damaged aircraft were successfully retrieved by being continually refueled until almost onto the carrier deck during the Vietnam conflict. A single trailing hose-drogue system mounted below the rear fuselage was also included for refueling U.S. Navy aircraft. The two additional wingtip-mounted drogue units proposed for the Canadian LRPA could also be used, but only the final production KC-10 incorporated these units. With the extra tanks located in the belly, the main deck was left unencumbered for the carriage of passengers or freight. The KC-10 could also receive fuel itself via a receptacle located above and behind the cockpit. It had already been tried out on the YC-15 experimental tactical transport that embodied the DC-10's cockpit section.

For the all-cargo role, the KC-10 utilizes a 10-foot by 21-foot, 8-inch cargo door on the left side. The forward lower cargo hold is accessible through a 66-inch by 104-inch-wide door on the right side, thus permitting rapid loading and unloading of the upper and lower decks. The rear cargo hold retains the standard DC-10CF door on the left side.

The U.S. Air Force's need for an air refueling tanker became more urgent in March 1975 when the new left-leaning Portuguese government

announced that C-141s carrying arms to Israel would not be allowed to refuel in the Azores. Most European countries had already refused overflights, further compounding the problem. This led the Air Force to ask Congress for $5.2 million to fund proposals from the three major manufacturers; a decision was to be made by July 1976. However, the TriStar was not seriously considered as it had limited fuel off-load capacity.

By November, Congress had approved the requested funding. Initial plans called for the Air Force to lease a DC-10 and Boeing 747, then modify both aircraft by installing additional fuel tanks and a boom system for aerial refueling. A six-month flight-testing program, flown by Air Force pilots, would then be undertaken. The estimated total cost was $60 million with the entire program completion to take 18 months. While the DC-10 never had a boom fitted, a series of flights using military aircraft of all types simulating refueling missions while closed-circuit video cameras monitored the operations. This exercise eventually led to the Royal Netherlands Air Force acquiring two ex-Martinair DC-10-30CFs in 1995. The aircraft were converted to tankers using a remote-controlled MDC boom, operated via closed-circuit television cameras.

Air Force planners also realized that these new tankers could support units of Tactical Air Command fighter-bombers on long flights without the need to land at intermediate foreign bases. This was subsequently

An F-14A from the U.S. Navy's Point Mugu Test Center plugs into the drogue system.

A "fish-eye" camera view of the KC-10 boom operator's control room.

The last production KC-10, AF87-0124 (ln 441/msn 48310), fitted with wingtip refueling pods. For flight testing, it was registered N6204N. (Tim Williams)

The boom operator's view of an SR-71 refueling. The reflection above the window is part of a two-mirror system to make the horizon visible for reference.

One of several Electronic Intelligence (EIInt) gathering proposals for the KC-10.

demonstrated when KC-10s refueled F-111s that attacked Libya from the United Kingdom. By flying over international waters, around France, Portugal and Spain no sovereign air space was entered. The KC-10s also allowed ferrying of fighter squadrons while carrying maintenance staff, ground support equipment and spares in the tanker.

The initial purchase plan was for the Air Force to issue formal Request for Proposals in August with responses due in November. A decision would be announced in April 1977 and an initial contract for five aircraft signed by late 1977. Three annual contracts for 12 aircraft would follow, subject to Congressional approval.

ATCA Win

The long drawn-out ATCA competition came to a head on December 19, 1977, when MDC was awarded an initial $28 million contract for production engineering, tooling and associated support based on an expected initial order for 20 KC-10s; others were to follow based on available funding. Appropriately named Extender, the KC-10 beat the Boeing 747 proposal in six different scenarios. One year later, on November 28, 1978, MDC received a formal contract for the first two KC-10s worth $132.5 million, plus a contract for spares and support systems valued at $15.5 million. The new boom was flight-tested on a Boeing KC-135 and proved far more efficient than the older system.

The initial KC-10 flight took place on July 12, 1980, with the first of many air-refueling tests following on October 30, 1980, when the KC-10's boom was plugged into a C-5A transport's receptacle 48 times during a four-and-one-half hour flight near Edwards AFB. The tests were carried out at 25,000 feet, cruising at a speed of 400 knots.

The first KC-10 delivery was made to the 32nd Aerial Refueling Squadron at Barksdale AFB, Louisiana on March 17, 1981. The second unit to receive the new tanker was the 722nd Aerial Refueling Wing (ARW) based at March AFB, California. Others went to the 68th ARW at Seymour Johnson AFB, North Carolina. The 60th aircraft was delivered on September 30, 1988.

Since that time, the Air Force has reorganized its commands and the KC-10s are currently based at only Travis AFB, California and McGuire AFB, New Jersey. At the time of writing, just one KC-10 has been lost, the result of an explosion on the flight line at Barksdale AFB in September 1987.

Wearing the "Shamu" camouflage introduced in the mid-1980s, KC-10 AF85-0027 (ln 402/msn 48232) tops off an SR-71.

The proposed KC-10 cruise-missile launch vehicle.

Other Air Force Proposals

In addition to the LRPA requirement for the Canadian Armed Forces and the air refueller for SAC, MDC began generating designs to modify DC-10s for other missions. The first studies were Electronic Intelligence Gathering (ElInt) models, which were designed in 1973. In 1976, details of a version capable of air-launching two Inter-Continental Ballistic Missiles (ICBMs) through a ventral door were released. A compressed air system was created to eject the missile tail first from its launch tube. When stabilized in an upright attitude by small thrusters, the rocket would ignite and fly a pre-programmed track to its target. Similar versions of other large transports were also under consideration as airborne launch vehicles.

A stand-off bomber version was proposed which utilized the lower cargo holds as bomb bays with doors in the belly. Each carried several Air Launched Cruise Missiles (ALCMs) similar to those used on today's larger jet bombers. The missiles would be ejected clear of the aircraft before the engines were started. Another study in 1978 showed fuselage-mounted rotary missile launchers, similar to a revolver, in blisters aft of the wings, which would eject the ALCMs down and away from the launcher before engine ignition. Sixty-four missiles could be carried in magazines of eight that moved on rails to the launch position.

Again, similar Air Force-funded studies were undertaken utilizing other jet transports. When the proposals were made public, there was a negative reaction from some airlines, which were concerned that the missile-launcher versions were indistinguishable from commercial airliners and could lead to airliner shoot-downs. Although Pentagon officials favored the concepts, the Air Force preferred purely military aircraft designs, so the idea was never consummated.

DC-10s were offered to the U.S. Air Force on three different occasions for Presidential use.

Between 1980 and 1982, MDC worked on a U.S. Air Force request for an Airborne Laser Platform (ALP) to intercept incoming long-range missiles in space, but funding ran out before the studies were completed. In 1988, the requirement was revived and the Boeing 747 selected as the vehicle to mount the system.

Air Force One

The Air Force issued a Request for Proposal in 1983 for two widebody aircraft to replace the VIP Boeing 707-320Bs. Funding of $300 million was budgeted to cover the two aircraft and their conversion to presidential configuration. The contract eventually went to the Boeing 747 when it was argued that four engines were safer than three, even though the DC-10 could operate from many more airports than its larger competitor. When the aircraft were finally delivered, the cost was more than $200 million each.

Super Guppy

In October 1984, at NASA's request, MDC engineers produced several studies to convert a KC-10 into a "Super Guppy" freighter. The requirement stemmed from a possible need to transport the Space Shuttle's payloads should it be forced make an emergency landing in West Africa. Although the modified Boeing 747 Shuttle Transporter could bring the spacecraft home in a series of short hops, it could not lift the combined weight of the Shuttle and its payload over an adequate distance. The

Artist's impression of a missile being ejected from a modified KC-10 ventral door.

Shuttle's payload capsule was to be transported in a canister 61 feet long and 15 feet in diameter, weighing 65,000 pounds.

MDC designers examined three versions, all with hinged cockpit sections so that the nose landing gear was unchanged. The initial study enlarged the forward fuselage, similar to the turboprop-powered Super Guppy, but this seriously affected the airflow to the rear engine. A second study retained the KC-10's cross-section but was stretched with a 279-inch plug ahead of the wing plus an aft 121-inch plug. The main floor was removed forward of the front spar, allowing the payload module to sit within the existing profile. However, this would have been an expensive conversion.

The final proposal was based on a similar approach that converted the old Douglas C-74 into the bulky C-124 Globemaster in the early 1950s. The upper fuselage was sliced off at the main deck floor line and an 80.5-inch high flat section was inserted down the full length of the aircraft. The MTOW remained at 580,000 pounds and the Operating Empty Weight was 250,600 pounds. With the Shuttle payload aboard, the range was 3,500 miles. However, the Air Force was loath to lose a valuable tanker asset, so the program was abandoned.

Clark Aircraft Corporation of Santa Barbara, California also proposed a similar approach in mid-1984 called the Advanced Aircargo Transport. This version also removed the main floor forward of the wing and hinged the nose. However, it did not feature a stretch and would have required 42,000 pounds of ballast or cargo to be carried in the aft belly cargo pit. A stretched version was offered, similar to the MDC concept with a 17-foot plug forward and a 10-foot plug aft. Like the MDC proposals, this approach did not come to fruition.

Converted Tankers

The only other air force to modify the DC-10 into a military tanker was the KLu, or Royal Netherlands Air Force. As mentioned earlier, two DC-10-30CFs were purchased from Martinair in 1995 and, with the assistance of MDC engineers, converted by KLM to KDC-10s. Utilizing the same boom system and belly tanks, the variant differs from the KC-10 by having the boom operator station located just aft of the cockpit. A series of belly-mounted cameras give the boom operator the same view the KC-10's operator sees. The two Dutch aircraft also incorporate the wingtip-mounted refueling pods equipped with the drogue system, but do not have the fuselage-mounted drogue system installed.

The two former Martinair DC-10-30CFs, converted into KDC-10s for the KLu by KLM. (Sgt1 Henk van Dijk, KLu)

The Airborne Laser system using the KC-10 as the platform.

Force Aerienne Belgique F-16s refuel from KDC-10 T-264 (In 264/msn 46985). The remote cameras are located in the bulge just forward of the boom mounting. (Sgt1 Henk van Dijk, KLu)

Nose Art

During the Desert Storm campaign of 1991, nose art appeared on many Coalition aircraft including KC-10s.

AF83-0779 (ln 390/msn 48220) aptly named *Shamu* after a camouflage pattern similar to the killer whale was applied.

AF84-0188 (ln 397/msn 48227) *Touch of Class* of the 722nd ARW at March AFB represents the tanker's capabilities.

Still in the original white-topped livery, *Great White* AF83-077 (ln 388/msn 48218).

AF79-1946 (ln 373/msn 48206) of the 9th ARS, 722nd ARW wears the squadron patch.

Appropriately registered, DC-10-30 9G-ANA (ln 369/msn 48286) in the original Ghana Airways livery.

The first flight of the DC-10-15 took place on January 8, 1981, the same day that the first DC-9-82 completed its maiden flight from the Yuma Test Center. Since the order had been placed, a number of improvements raised the MTOW to 455,000 pounds and increased fuel capacity.

Ghana announced a DC-10-30 purchase for 1982 delivery on January 5. Finnair became the only other airline to buy a new Series 30ER, its third DC-10, and Lufthansa placed an order for its last DC-10 on January 22. Finnair also stated that it would retrofit its existing two aircraft to the same standard for the 6,000-mile route from Helsinki to Tokyo. Several other airlines retrofitted DC-10s to the DC-10-30ER standard. During January, British Caledonian introduced main-deck baggage stowage on four aircraft assigned to the North Atlantic routes in an effort to increase cargo capacity.

End of a Legend

Sadly, Donald Wills Douglas Sr. passed away on February 1, 1981, at a hospital in Palm Springs, California; he was 88 years old. Mr. Douglas founded the original Douglas Aircraft Company in 1920 and, at the time of his death, was still Chairman Emeritus of the McDonnell Douglas Corporation.

Used Aircraft Glut

In March, 34 used DC-10s were available for sale, mostly by the Asian and Pacific carriers. Continental and Western were also prepared to sell aircraft and World Airways, in financial trouble, offered its fleet for sale. Sixteen TriStars and numerous Boeing 747s were also on offer.

At the end of March, MDC and American reached a settlement regarding payments to families of the victims from the Chicago crash, but details were never revealed. A few weeks earlier, a Federal Appeals panel had absolved MDC of any liability or punitive damages arising from the accident.

DC-10 deliveries reached 343 out of the 366 firm plus 20 options by the end of June. Among these, the first Series 15 was accepted by Mexicana on June 15, in a 315-seat, single-class configuration, three days after the FAA issued its type certificate.

Subleased from Shabair, DC-10-30 9G-PHN (ln 84/msn 46554) in 1990s white. (Author's Collection)

Flight Testing Winglets

MDC leased Continental's DC-10-10 N68048 (ln 101/msn 47802) for the winglet flight-test program.

In the late 1970s, NASA sponsored analytical studies by McDonnell Douglas and Boeing to investigate the benefits of installing winglets on the DC-10 and Boeing 747. The initial results looked so promising to MDC and NASA that they decided to conduct a brief program to flight test several winglet versions. NASA contributed $11 million to the project.

A DC-10-10 was leased back from Continental Airlines in early 1981. Its wingtips were modified to accept several different winglet configurations. The test units were constructed of aluminum, wood and fiberglass. Temporary stiffening of the outer wing panels was required in order to reduce wing bending; this was accomplished by adding more stiffeners to the existing upper wing stiffeners.

The first flight with winglets departed from Long Beach on August 31, 1981, following a series of flights in the standard configuration to establish a baseline. The initial winglets stood 10.5 feet above the wing and were flown with and without 2.5-foot extensions below the wing. Subsequent flights were also flown with the upper winglet height reduced to seven feet. In all cases the upper winglets were angled out at 75 degrees and the lower sections angled at 36 degrees from the horizontal.

Some tests were flown with a fixed Krueger flap fitted to the winglet leading edges with the flap-angle setting adjusted on the ground. They were added because analytical studies indicated that the winglet might stall at high angles of attack during the low-speed conditions associated with second-segment climbs. Subsequently, the Krueger flaps were considered to be unnecessary. Various leading-edge extensions were also briefly tested and discarded.

A total of 151 flight test hours were flown during 49 flights; the last flight occurred on October 28, 1981. Most of the testing was based at MDC's Yuma Flight Test facility although a few initial flights to determine flutter conditions were also flown from Edwards AFB. During most tests, the winglets covered with tufts to enable filming of the airflow patterns. The tests confirmed that a combination of upper and lower winglets improved the cruise lift-drag performance by between 1.5 and 2 percent with similar savings in fuel burn.

The shorter winglet appeared to be the best suited for the DC-10 wing but retrofitting was not considered attractive because of the increased wing bending and the need to strengthen the outer wing panels. The winglets were to be incorporated in the proposed Super DC-10 and, of course, eventually appeared on the MD-11.

A series of wind tunnel tests completed in February 1982 indicated that fitting Series 30 wing extensions to the Series 10 matched the figures obtained during the winglet trials.

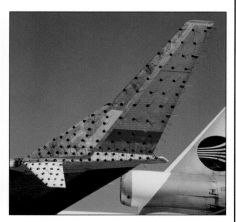

Both 6- and 10-foot high winglets were test flown, with and without the lower vane. Fixed Krueger flaps, adjustable on the ground, and extended leading-edge variations were also tested. Tufts permit filming of the airflows.

General Slowdown

In addition to the earlier orders, MDC had 12 KC-10s on the books and had recently started deliveries. From 40 aircraft delivered 1980, the number fell to just 26 in 1981. No firm orders existed for 1983 except for four KC-10s, but there were still 17 options on the books. The situation looked worse when the Reagan administration announced that it was thinking of canceling the remaining eight KC-10s on order due to budgetary restraints.

Across the city, Lockheed had been building TriStars at a rate of 28 per year, but was in the process of tapering down to 18. Its forecast rate for 1983 was one per month. All were built at a loss due to old contract terms, inefficient production rates and high inflation. Adding to Lockheed's woes, Pan Am requested delayed deliveries of two TriStar 500s due to financial difficulties. Pan Am also put four DC-10s on the market and, in an effort to help out, the airline's pilots tried to arrange financing to buy three of them to form an employee-owned, low-cost charter airline. But Pan Am's board rejected the idea as it would have drained low-yield traffic from the parent airline. Even Boeing 747 production was declining and the Boeing 727 was dropping from 11 per month to six.

In early September, the U.S. Federal Appeals Court ruled that the FAA had violated the Chicago Convention when it had banned foreign-registered DC-10s from U.S. airspace. This ruling cleared the way for the European airlines to sue the FAA for lost revenue during the grounding. British Caledonian was the first to file suit claiming damages of $1.84 million for loss of revenue.

More Problems

An Air Florida DC-10 taking off from Miami experienced a burst engine just prior to rotation on September 22, but abandoned the takeoff. Once again, the leading-edge slats suffered considerable damage from shrapnel, causing a dissimilar slat setting. Back in April 1977, a PIA DC-10 suffered a similar occurrence at 400 feet just after takeoff. Fortunately, it had reached sufficient speed to continue the climb out, circle, dump fuel and land at a higher than normal speed. MDC had already modified the slat hydraulic systems after the O'Hare accident, but made further changes to ensure that slats would remain in identical positions via a series of check valves and springs. Now, new modifications were added to allow outer sections of the slats to still function should the more damage-prone inner sections be damaged.

The DC-10 Super 10

By October 1, 1981, only 19 aircraft – including the eight KC-10s – remained on order. Contracts in 1982 called for 14 deliveries so MDC embarked on a major campaign to prevent cancellation of the KC-10 order and save the DC-10 program.

Attempting to extend the DC-10 production run, MDC showed 17 potential customers a new model of the aircraft known as the DC-10 Super 10. This was a Series 10 re-engined with either P&W 2037 engines rated at 39,000 pounds of thrust, the Rolls Royce RB.211-535F4s rated at 40,600 pounds of thrust or the 45,000-pound-thrust GE CF6-80 power plants. The PW2037 was the engine of choice as it was lighter and physically smaller than the two competitors; having a new nacelle and pylon for the wing engines would further reduce drag. Installation of winglets and a new flight management system were expected to help decrease fuel consumption by 20 percent per seat-mile and lower the direct operating costs by about 14 percent. It would equal the performance of earlier Series 30 and 40 versions at the much lower MTOW of 455,000 pounds. A second shortened model reduced seat rows by two but came with a longer range to match the newer DC-10s. Later studies traded the winglets for the Series 30's wingtip extensions.

Stretched DC-10 Super 10 studies added six more seat rows by inserting a 100-inch plug ahead of the wing and a 121-inch addition just behind it. Engine choice lay between the GE CF6-80C1 rated at 60,000 pounds of thrust or the 56,000-pounds thrust P&W JT9D-7R4H. Both models retained the Series 30/40 wing. Delivery was aimed at mid-1985, depending on engine selection. MDC also examined a rework package to convert Series 10s to Super 10s.

Lockheed's board formally announced termination of TriStar production during the first week of December. The 250th and final L-1011 would be finished in August 1983; the last five were built on speculation and sold during 1984 and 1985.

The year 1981 ended on a low note for MDC with still no DC-10s on order for 1983 delivery, although the intense lobbying for the KC-10 showed signs of working, and four additional 1983 deliveries were being proposed in Congress.

Brochure illustration of the proposed DC-10 Super 10 offered to British Airways.

Finally, the U.S. Air Force confirmed an order for four more KC-10s and JAL also ordered a Series 40 on January 18, 1982, bringing its total to 20. The future looked even brighter on January 28 when the Pentagon asked Congress to approve funding for an additional 44 KC-10s to be delivered over a five-year period; this would bring the KC-10 fleet to a total to 60.

Laker's Problems

Early in the winter of 1981-82, North Atlantic traffic fell off dramatically. Pan Am, in deep financial trouble, matched the Laker Skytrain fares and other carriers followed suit just as bad weather along the U.S. East Coast reduced tourist traffic to almost nil. Laker had recently taken delivery of the first three of 10 A-300s, ordered for a proposed low-fare scheduled European operation. Unfortunately, strong opposition from all the existing scheduled carriers stopped Laker from operating the A-300s except in charter services, putting the airline into a serious cash flow situation.

MDC and GE offered additional funding and a new payment schedule, but the financial institutions and Airbus Industrie, both under pressure from the European flag carriers, refused to help. MDC and GE suddenly realized that any investment would result in part ownership, which was illegal under United States law. So, on February 6, 1982, by now Sir Freddy Laker had no option but to call in the receivers and cease operations.

Later, Laker's U.S. attorney used the Freedom of Information Act to access Pan Am's filings with the CAB. Among the documents obtained were three sets of IATA meeting minutes that proved that several major airlines had conspired to put Laker out of business. Sir Freddy eventually received a substantial damage settlement.

Two of the Laker Series 10s were snapped up by British Caledonian for charter work and the others were placed in storage. MDC took a $50-million pre-tax loss from the Laker financing. Five of the Series 30s belonged to the Export-Import Bank as primary mortgage holder. These were offered to the U.S. Air Force for several missions, but all were abandoned due to lack of available funding.

In December 1982, four of the aircraft were also offered to the RAF to fulfill an aerial refueling tanker requirement exposed after the Falklands campaign. This bid was made in conjunction with British Caledonian, which would have maintained the aircraft, and British Aerospace, where conversion work would have been completed. Although the RAF preferred DC-10s, it eventually lost to BA's offer of its six TriStar 500s following substantial lobbying. The TriStar deal created considerable controversy when the airline – in debt for $1.5 billion – sold some of its newest aircraft for less than half the purchase price and recorded a book loss of more than $100 million on the transaction.

New Name

To establish its correct corporate identity, the DC-10 Super 10 was renamed MD-EEE (Economy, Ecology and Efficiency) in August. Similarly, the DC-9 Super 80 was re-branded as the MD-80. The Super 10 Series 30's 5-foot per side wing extensions were retained and initially the engines were unchanged, but Rolls-Royce offered a new version of the RB.211, the 535H4 rated at 41,500 pounds of thrust, to power it. The MTOW was raised to 475,000 pounds, including 190,230 pounds of fuel. The 237,000-pound Operating Empty Weight (OEW) was 10,000 pounds lighter than the Series 10 because much of the secondary structure was to be made from composite materials. Twenty-two first-class and 248 economy-class passengers plus baggage could be carried 5,200 miles, about the same as a Series 30 but using 21 percent less fuel. The two-man cockpit was equipped with advanced digital avionics.

The stretched MD-EEE study added a 100-inch plug forward of the wing and 121-inch increase aft; seating 30 in first-class and 294 in economy-class. The only other change was the addition of drooped

inboard ailerons to reduce field-length requirements. The higher OEW of 256,285 pounds reduced the range to 4,200 miles. A great deal of negotiating with several Japanese companies to co-share in the production of major subassemblies failed to elicit any interest.

The Pentagon announced confirmation of the 44 KC-10 order for $2.7 billion on December 30, with deliveries spread through 1988. This was welcome news as just five commercial DC-10s and six KC-10s had been delivered during the year. Three others were built and stored due to financial or political delays.

Yet Another Option

In early 1983, Pratt & Whitney's PW 4000 power plant, GE's CF6-80C2 and the RB.211-600 were offered for 1986 certification. All were in the 55,000- to 60,000-pound-thrust class. MDC incorporated these new engines into yet another series of models known as the MD-100. Five versions were developed as follows:-

SERIES	-10	-20	-10ER	-20 COMBI	-30
Cabin Length *(Ft)*	Base	+26.7	Base	+26.7	+45
Seats *(2-Class)*	270	333	270	*221	387
MTOW *(1,000 lb)*	500	580	580	580	580
Range*(n.m.)*	5,650	5,740	7,000	*4,200	4,500
Year Available	1987	1988	1989	1989-90	1989-90

* With space-limited payload (10 lbs/cu ft) including six 88-inch by 125-inch main-deck pallets.

All of the models embodied the MD-EEE upgrades except for the engines, introduction of winglets (increasing the span to 169 feet) and the "Chisel" rear fuselage fairing which reduced drag. The -20 version had three plugs fitted 60 inches behind the cockpit, 140 inches ahead of the wing and 121 inches aft of the wing.

The program failed to garner interest mainly because improved large power plant reliability was about to make twin-engine trans-Atlantic flying viable.

Throughout 1983, deliveries were mainly KC-10s, with eight handed over that year. The four commercial deliveries included two Series 15s for Mexicana in January that had previously been held up pending financing arrangements. Ghana's Series 30 was delivered in May after being held up by a revolution in that country. JAL also took its last aircraft in March; it was the 367th commercial DC-10 to be delivered. It was slightly delayed too, having been the first DC-10 with the new Performance Management System that reduced fuel burn by up to 3 percent. This system was also installed in one KC-10 and subsequently added to the entire tanker fleet.

In November, Pan Am and American entered into an agreement whereby American would trade its eight Boeing 747s to Pan Am in exchange for 15 DC-10s in a fleet rationalization move. The Italian Air Force also looked into buying a used Series 30CF to convert to a tanker/transport, but lack of funding killed the project.

The MD-XXX

MDC introduced a new MD-XXX study in early 1984. Offered in two versions, standard and stretched, the MTOW was 580,000 pounds with either PW4000 or GE CF6-50C2 engines. An extended tail cone and two-position leading-edge slats were also included. The MD-XXX differed from the MD-100 by retaining the DC-10's three-man cockpit to reduce development time and cost. The stretched version was the same size as the MD-100-20. The basic aircraft had a range of 6,480 miles with 270 passengers, while the stretched version would carry 331 passengers 5,710 miles. Fuel burn per seat was 16 percent less than the standard Series 30. Fuel savings with the stretch would be 24 percent. Because of the simpler changes, deliveries could have been made in 1988. In October, the project was re-named MD-11X.

126

Delivered in January 1986, FedEx DC-10-30F N306FE (In 409/msn 48287) wears its original colors.

FedEx to the Rescue

In early May, FedEx signed two purchase agreements with MDC. The first was for a DC-10-30CF that had been built in 1980 for Lauda Air and stored after the deal fell through. FedEx briefly considered operating the

Zambia's first DC-10-30 N3016Z (In 348/msn 48266) was leased for 10 years starting in July 1984. A second aircraft, 9J-AFN (In 122/msn 47922), below, was an intended lease from Lufthansa in 1990, but never consummated.

aircraft during the week as a freighter and carrying charter passengers on palletized seating at the weekends. However, concerns about potential delays scuttled the idea. The aircraft was delivered in September in freighter mode. The second contract was for five DC-10-30Fs for 1986 delivery. These differed from the CFs by having higher cabin ceilings to increase the volume and deletion of all passenger-related items. Powered by GE CF6-50C2s, the MTOW was 580,000 pounds with a maximum payload of 172,000 pounds.

Zambia Airways took delivery of a DC-10-30 in August. Stored since 1982 after the contract with Egyptair fell through, it was sold for $45 million including spares, training and other support. After the unpublicized Letter of Intent was signed in mid-1983, the financing package became the most complicated ever conceived, involving 11 banks in seven countries; it was completed just days prior to acquisition. The remaining eight deliveries in 1984 were all KC-10s.

Missile Attack

During the September Russian invasion of Afghanistan, Ariana's DC-10 was struck in the left wing and engine by a shoulder-launched missile while landing at Kabul, but there were no injuries. The aircraft was ferried to Frankfurt where an MDC team repaired it. Early in 1985, the Russian occupiers forced the airline to sell the DC-10 (to British Caledonian) and replace it with Tu-154s.

Final Sales

FedEx ordered three more DC-10-30Fs on July 31, 1985, with deliveries scheduled for early in 1988. This brought remaining deliveries to eight for FedEx plus 28 KC-10s. However, FedEx subsequently canceled the last two deliveries as it was building up its DC-10 fleet by buying used aircraft from several airlines. MDC was able to sell the canceled aircraft, reconfigured in passenger configuration, to Biman Bangladesh in December 1988 and Nigeria Airways in July 1989.

Production in 1985 consisted of just 11 KC-10s. Meanwhile, United contracted with Tracor at Santa Barbara, California to modify all its Series 30s by relocating the lower galleys to the main deck to increase cargo capacity. Several other airlines followed suit.

The first of five DC-10-30Fs delivered to FedEx in 1986 was handed over on January 24 and further KC-10 deliveries were also completed. By now, the sales department was concentrating its efforts in launching the MD-11, but did manage to sell two Series 30ERs to Thai International with deliveries in mid-1988. A surprise sale was to Toa Domestic Airlines (TDA), which bought two Series 30s. The airline changed its name to Japan Air System on April 2, 1988, two days after the first aircraft, already in the new livery,

Bangladesh Biman initially acquired used DC-10-30s. However, its last aircraft, S2-ACR (ln 445/msn 48317), was bought new. It is shown wearing test registration N6203U. (Tim Williams)

Japan Air System (JAS) operated two Series 30s, including JA8551 (ln 437/msn 48316) rather than the Series 40s selected by JAL.

JA8550 (ln 436/msn 48315) was assigned to the JAS charter subsidiary, Harlequin Air in 1998. (Avimage)

A picture worth a million words. The first MD-11 dwarfs its predecessor, the Douglas DC-2 of 1934.

was delivered. The last sale was to Thai International, which bought its third Series 30ER for May 1988 delivery. The remainder of the KC-10 deliveries continued throughout 1987 and the last was handed over on September 30, 1988, though it was leased back to MDC for a short while to flight test the wingtip-mounted refueling pods.

The MD-11

The design engineers' efforts to continually refine the basic DC-10 design finally came to fruition in October 1985 when board approval was given to start negotiations with a number of airlines for the MD11X – later re-designated MD-11 – and the design was frozen at last.

Many modern innovations were introduced into the specification. While the aircraft retained a similarity to the DC-10, the fuselage was stretched 18 feet, 6 inches, and winglets were added. The horizontal tail was reduced in area and incorporated fuel tanks with a stability augmentation system that transfers fuel to these tanks to improve the balance. The outer panels of the mainplane were aft-loaded to improve aerodynamic and range performance. The MTOW was established at 602,500 pounds.

The two-person cockpit, known as the Advanced Common Flightdeck, was fitted with flat-panel computer displays and dual flight-management systems plus an automatic flight-control system. In the cabin, the lavatory

The first MD-10F (N386FE, ln 138/msn 46220) begins its maiden flight at Long Beach on April 10, 1999. It was originally United's Series 10 N1821U.

systems featured a vacuum type waste disposal system and the cabin layout was designed for rapid reconfiguration of seating, lavatories and other modules. Both the GE CF6-50C2 and PW4000 engines were offered with little difference in performance. As usual, several versions were on offer, depending on range requirements.

The board required a minimum of 20 orders with production start slated for late 1987. As a drive to sell the MD-11 gathered pace, efforts to sell the DC-10 tapered off. The last aircraft, for Nigeria Airways, was delivered on July 27, 1989, just over 30 years since production of the first DC-10 had started.

MD-10

As newer aircraft came along, DC-10s were inevitably withdrawn from passenger service and a few were converted to freighters. FedEx perceived the DC-10-10 as an ideal transcontinental freighter. The cargo airline already had an agreement to purchase 36 United Airlines Series 10s as they became available and had started negotiating with American for most of its fleet. Unfortunately, some of the aircraft had already been dismantled for spares and scrap.

On September 18, 1996, FedEx reached agreement with MDC for a two-stage program to convert 60 Series 10s to MD-10 standards. The first stage included conversion of the aircraft to basic freighters. Part two was the installation of the two-person Advanced Common Flightdeck. This not only increased efficiency, but brought the aircraft in line with the fleet of

MD-11 Freighters that FedEx had acquired after the end of DC-10 production. Contracts were signed with several conversion specialists. Design and conversion of the prototype aircraft was undertaken at Long Beach by MDC – later Boeing – in August 1997. In the meantime, the number of conversion orders was increased to 79 with options for another 40. The first MD-10 flight took place on   April 10, 1999. A second aircraft followed in early September with full certification and initial deliveries scheduled to begin in March 2000.

Northwest and Continental acquired many used Series 30s, while others were converted to all-cargo configuration by their operators. The Series 15s were bought by Skyjet for wet-leases to small airlines. Japan Airlines' Series 40s are being converted for cargo use by several carriers, including Challenge Air. Interestingly, FedEx didn't actively seek any used Series 30s, presumably because the MD-11s are ideal for most of its long-haul routes and the Series 10s for U.S. domestic routes where the Series 30 – with its higher weights and fuel burn – offer no additional volume.

Several DC-10s have exceeded 100,000 hours of their expected 120,000-hour lives. Among the highest is a Series 30, N220NW (ln 114/msn 46577) operated by Northwest. It had logged more than 107,000 hours by September 1999. Two Series 10s have completed more than 31,000 of their 40,000-landing design lives. However, the bulk of the fleet are considered barely midlife aircraft and should be on the cargo scene for many years to come.

The cockpit of the MD-10 is identical to the MD-11Fs of FedEx and looks quite modern when compared with that of the original DC-10 (page 40).

AOM operates services for other carriers. DC-10-30 F-ODLX (ln 233/msn 46872) appears with Cubana and, below, Africa West Air titles.

British Caledonian DC-10-30 G-BEBM (ln 214/msn 46921), wet-leased to Caribbean Airways in 1982. (Author's Collection)

TAINO, a Dominican airline, subleased DC-10-30 F-GHOI (ln 217/msn 46870) from Scribe in 1993. (via Eddy Gual)

TAESA operated some services for Dominicana with DC-10-30 XA-SYE (ln 260/msn 46990) in 1995-96. (via Eddy Gual)

Series 30CF XA-TDC (ln 127/msn 46891) serves New SouthWays. (via Eddy Gual)

Used in 1998 Hadj operations, Laker DC-10-30 N831LA (ln 147/msn 46936) flew as Transmile Air, a Malaysian company. (Avimage)

TAROM, Romania's airline, subleased DC-10-30 OO-JOT (ln 63/msn 46850) from Challenge Air in 1995. (Author's Collection)

Skyjet, a Belgian airline, specializes in short-term leases. Recent DC-10-15 Hadj flights included V2-LER (ln 372/msn 48294) for Guinee Airlines. (Avimage)

PP-OOO (ln 346/msn 48258) was operated on behalf of Saudi Arabian. (African Slide Service)

V2-LER (ln 372/msn 48294) flew for Air Afrique. (Exavia)

Temporary stickers applied for a few trips are not unusual. Above, KLM DC-10-30 PH-DTD (ln 82/msn 46553) operates a flight for Kenya Airways. Below, Martinair DC-10-30CF PH-MBT (ln 264/msn 46985) sporting the Air Seychelles name.

During the summer of 1997, Caledonian leased Series 30 OO-LRM (ln 63/msn 46850) for the season from Challenge Air. (Author's Collection)

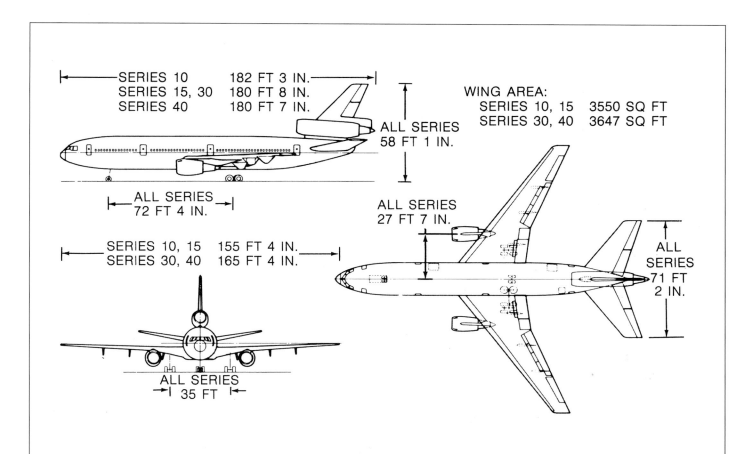

SERIES 10   182 FT 3 IN.
SERIES 15, 30   180 FT 8 IN.
SERIES 40   180 FT 7 IN.

WING AREA:
SERIES 10, 15   3550 SQ FT
SERIES 30, 40   3647 SQ FT

ALL SERIES 58 FT 1 IN.

ALL SERIES 72 FT 4 IN.

ALL SERIES 27 FT 7 IN.

SERIES 10, 15   155 FT 4 IN.
SERIES 30, 40   165 FT 4 IN.

ALL SERIES 71 FT 2 IN.

ALL SERIES 35 FT

		SERIES 10	SERIES 15	SERIES 30	SERIES 40
S	ENGINE	CF6-6D	CF6-50C2F	CF6-50C	JT9D-59A
T	THRUST (LB)	40,000	46,500	51,000	53,000
A	MTOGW (LB)	430,000	455,000	555,000	555,000
N	MLW (LB)	363,500	363,500	403,000	403,000
D	MZFW (LB)	335,000	335,000	368,000	368,000
A	OEW (LB)	245,467	247,252	267,996	271,848
R	PASSENGERS	275	275	277	277
D	FUEL CAPACITY (LB)	145,810	145,810	245,566	245,579

		SERIES 10	SERIES 15	SERIES 30	SERIES 40
O	ENGINE	CF6-6D1	—	CF6-50C2B	JT9D-59B
P	THRUST (LB)	41,000	—	54,000	54,000
T	MTOGW (LB)	455,000	—	580,000	580,000
I	MLW (LB)	367,500	367,500	436,000	436,000
O	MZFW (LB)	342,500	342,500	414,000	414,000
N	PASSENGERS	UP TO 380	UP TO 380	UP TO 380	UP TO 380
S	ADDITIONAL FUEL (LB)	32,700	32,700	21,400	21,400

Appendix II
WRITE-OFFS

Airline	Model	Registration	ln/msn	Date	Comments
Iberia	30	EC-CBN	087/46925	12/17/73	Undershoot landing; Boston
THY	10	TC-JAV	029/46704	03/03/74	Explosive decompression near Paris
ONA	30CF	N1032F	109/46826	11/12/75	Bird strike on takeoff; New York
ONA	30CF	N1031F	081/46825	01/02/76	Landed short at Istanbul
Continental	10	N68045	044/46904	03/01/78	Tire burst; aborted takeoff; Los Angeles
American	10	N110AA	022/46510	05/25/79	Engine separated on takeoff; Chicago
Western	10	N903WA	107/46929	10/31/79	Landed on closed runway; Mexico City
Air New Zealand	30	ZK-NZP	182/46910	11/28/79	Hit Mt. Erebus in white-out; Antarctica
PIA	30	AP-AXE	172/46935	02/03/81	Caught fire at Karachi
World Airways	30CF	N113WA	320/47821	01/23/82	Skidded off icy runway; Boston
Spantax	30CF	EC-DEG	238/46962	09/13/82	Tire burst; aborted takeoff; Malaga
Korean	30F	HL7339	237/46960	12/23/83	Hit light aircraft on takeoff; Anchorage
ATA	10	N184AT	038/46751	08/10/86	Caught fire at Chicago
USAF	KC-10	82-0192	384/48214	09/17/87	On-ground explosion; Barksdale AFB
Nigeria	30	5N-ANR	243/46968	01/10/87	Caught fire on training flight; Ilorin, Nigeria
American	30	N136AA	069/47846	05/21/88	Aborted takeoff; Dallas
United	10	N1819U	118/46618	07/19/89	No. 2 engine failure; crashed at Sioux City, Iowa
Korean	30	HL7328	125/47887	07/27/89	Crashed on approach in fog; Tripoli
UTA	30	N54629	093/46852	09/19/89	Terrorist bomb explosion over Niger
Martinair	30CF	PH-MBN	218/46924	12/21/92	Heavy landing; Faro, Portugal
American	30	N139AA	105/46711	04/14/93	Heavy landing; Dallas
Garuda	30	PK-GIE	284/46685	06/13/96	Engine failure; aborted takeoff; Fukuoka, Japan
FedEx	10F	N68055	191/47809	09/05/96	In-flight cargo fire
Cubana	30	F-GTDI	077/46890	12/21/99	Overran runway on landing; Guatemala City

The American Transair DC-10-40 N184AT (ln 36/msn 46751) at O'Hare on August 10, 1986. The fire was caused by mishandled oxygen by cabin cleaning crews. (Ron Kluk)

PRODUCTION LIST

This table contains data reported to Boeing through September 1999. Where flight hours only are reported, the aircraft was still reporting monthly activity.

The individual aircraft information which follows is sequenced in order of actual production, by Line Number (LN). The manufacturer's serial number (MSN) formally identifies the airframe for legal purposes and remains constant throughout its life. A formal plate is permanently fixed to the forward entry doorjamb on the left side.

Registration (REG), Airline (A/L), MODEL and Engine (ENG) columns show the status at the time of delivery. Model numbers are explained in the text. Delivery dates (DEL) are those on which the aircraft title was transferred to the airline or its lending company. Title transfer is recorded at the precise moment when final payment is deposited in the manufacturer's account, allowing insurance liability to be transferred as well.

The Status (STAT) column indicates whether the aircraft is Retired (RET), stored (STO) or was written off (W/0). For aircraft still active, the Status and Date columns are left blank.

Retired aircraft dates indicate when the manufacturer was formally notified of the status change. However, in some cases, the final flight may pre-date this. Flight hours (HOURS) include final figures for DC-10s no longer flying.

Many DC-10s are in the process of being – or have been – converted to all-cargo configurations that change the designation. This is shown in the last column (CVTD). Most of the DC-10-10s owned by FedEx are scheduled to be converted to MD-10s and are identified with an asterisk. The notation SPL refers to those airframes that received other, non-standard conversions, including ln 002 (Project Orbis), ln 065, (Raytheon Company) and ln 157 (Minebea Technologies).

AIRLINE (A/L) ABBREVIATIONS – ORIGINAL DELIVERY CUSTOMERS

AA	American Airlines
AM	Aeronaves de Mexico
AY	Finnair
AZ	Alitalia
BG	Bangladesh Biman
BR	British Caledonian Airways
CO	Continental Airlines
CP	CP Air
DL	Delta Air Lines
FG	Ariana Afghan Airlines
FM	Federal Express Corp.
GA	Garuda Indonesian Airlines
GH	Ghana Airways
GK	Laker Airways
IB	Iberia
JL	Japan Air Lines
JU	Jugoslav Air Transport (JAT)
KE	Korean Air Lines
KL	KLM Royal Dutch Airlines
LH	Lufthansa
MH	Malaysian Airlines System
MX	Mexicana
NA	National Airlines
NW	Northwest Orient Airlines
OV	Overseas National Airlines
PK	Pakistan International Airlines
PR	Philippine Air Lines
QC	Air Zaire
QZ	Zambia Airways
RG	Varig
RK	Air Afrique
SK	Scandinavian Airlines System (SAS)
SN	Sabena Belgian World Airlines
SQ	Singapore Airlines
SR	Swissair
TE	Air New Zealand
TG	Thai International Airways
TK	Turkish Airlines
TV	Trans International Airlines
UA	United Air Lines
UT	UTA
VA	Viasa
WA	Western Airlines
WD	Wardair (Canada) Ltd
WO	World Airways
WT	Nigerian Airways
YM	Martinair
YB	Balair
YD	Condor
YV	Air Siam
ZA	United States Air Force

LN	MSN	REG	A/L	MODEL	ENG	DEL	STAT	HOURS	DATE	CVTD
001	46500	N101AA	AA	10	CF6-6D	12-08-72		063,328		10F*
002	46501	G-BELO	GK	10	CF6-6D1	06-03-77		036,008		SPL
003	46502	N102AA	AA	10	CF6-6D	06-27-72		061,444		10F*
004	46600	N1801U	UA	10	CF6-6D	05-25-72		062,131		10F*
005	46503	N103AA	AA	10	CF6-6D	07-29-71		062,351		10F*
006	46601	N1802U	UA	10	CF6-6D	07-29-71		065,411		10F*
007	46504	N104AA	AA	10	CF6-6D	09-17-71	RET	061,912	09-14-95	
008	46602	N1803U	UA	10	CF6-6D	06-03-72		061,796		10F*
009	46505	N105AA	AA	10	CF6-6D	11-09-71		062,795		10F*
010	46603	N1804U	UA	10	CF6-6D	09-07-71	RET	060,703	09-07-93	
011	46604	N1805U	UA	10	CF6-6D	10-29-71	RET	061,030	09-07-93	
012	46506	N106AA	AA	10	CF6-6D	12-10-71		062,688		10F*
013	46507	N107AA	AA	10	CF6-6D	12-15-71		062,518		10F*
014	46700	N60NA	NA	10	CF6-6D	11-01-71	STO	067,506	1998	
015	46605	N1806U	UA	10	CF6-6D	12-23-71		062,698		10F*

LN	MSN	REG	A/L	MODEL	ENG	DEL	STAT	HOURS	DATE	CVTD
016	46701	N61NA	NA	10	CF6-6D	11-19-71		068,777		10F*
017	46606	N1807U	UA	10	CF6-6D	12-20-71		062,742		10F*
018	46702	N62NA	NA	10	CF6-6D	12-21-71	RET	071,300	08-15-97	
019	46703	N63NA	NA	10	CF6-6D	01-12-72		081,116		
020	46508	N108AA	AA	10	CF6-6D	01-31-72		062,027		10F*
021	46509	N109AA	AA	10	CF6-6D	01-21-72	RET	062,402	03-10-95	
022	46510	N110AA	AA	10	CF6-6D	02-28-72	W/O	019,871	05-25-79	
023	46511	N111AA	AA	10	CF6-6D	03-15-72	RET	061,753	05-31-93	
024	46512	N112AA	AA	10	CF6-6D	03-30-72		060,397		10F*
025	46607	N1808U	UA	10	CF6-6D	02-27-72		061,793		10F*
026	46608	N1809U	UA	10	CF6-6D	02-29-72		060,822		10F*
027	46609	N1810U	UA	10	CF6-6D	04-20-72		070,463		10F*
028	46750	N141US	NW	40	JT9D-20	06-13-73		074,399		
029	46704	TC-JAV	TK	10	CF6-6D	12-10-72	W/O	002,953	03-04-74	
030	46513	N113AA	AA	10	CF6-6D	04-20-72	RET	060,595	07-05-93	
031	46514	N114AA	AA	10	CF6-6D	05-17-72	RET	060,729	06-12-96	
032	46610	N1811U	UA	10	CF6-6D	04-24-72		071,571		
033	46705	TC-JAU	TK	10	CF6-6D	12-02-72		040,487		10F*
034	46900	N68041	CO	10	CF6-6D	04-14-72		084,956		10F
035	46611	N1812U	UA	10	CF6-6D	04-27-72		070,885		10F*
036	46751	N142US	NW	40	JT9D-20	02-16-73	W/O	029,155	08-10-86	
037	46515	N115AA	AA	10	CF6-6D	05-26-72		061,586		10F*
038	46706	N64NA	NA	10	CF6-6D	05-10-72		070,710		10F
039	46612	N1813U	UA	10	CF6-6D	05-27-72		070,910		
040	46901	N68042	CO	10	CF6-6D	05-22-72		085,998		10F
041	46902	N68043	CO	10	CF6-6D	05-19-72		086,330		10F
042	46613	N1814U	UA	10	CF6-6D	06-23-72		070,423		10F*
043	46903	N68044	CO	10	CF6-6D	06-09-72		086,265		
044	46904	N68045	CO	10	CF6-6D	06-23-72	W/O	021,358	03-01-78	
045	46614	N1815U	UA	10	CF6-6D	07-07-72		071,534		
046	46550	PH-DTA	KL	30	CF6-50A	03-15-74		091,337		
047	46905	G-AZZC	GK	10	CF6-6D1	10-26-72	RET	056,826	07-24-97	
048	46516	N116AA	AA	10	CF6-6D	07-14-72		081,911		10F*
049	46517	N117AA	AA	10	CF6-6D	07-21-72		066,625		10F*
050	46906	G-AZZD	GK	10	CF6-6D1	11-16-72		072,697		
051	46518	N118AA	AA	10	CF6-6D	07-29-72		066,218		10F*
052	46519	N119AA	AA	10	CF6-6D	08-11-72		081,125		
053	46752	N143US	NW	40	JT9D-20	11-10-72		064,621		
054	46520	N120AA	AA	10	CF6-6D	08-24-72		065,306		10F*
055	46521	N121AA	AA	10	CF6-6D	09-01-72		065,901		10F*
056	46522	N122AA	AA	10	CF6-6D	09-18-72		081,290		
057	46575	HB-IHA	SR	30	CF6-50A	11-30-72		088,204		
058	46523	N123AA	AA	10	CF6-6D	10-20-72		068,082		
059	47965	N601DA	DL	10	CF6-6D	10-10-72		075,338		10F*
060	46551	PH-DTB	KL	30	CF6-50A	12-03-72		101,336		
061	46707	N65NA	NA	10	CF6-6D	10-13-72		079,059		
062	46708	N66NA	NA	10	CF6-6D	10-19-72		077,064		
063	46850	F-BTDB	UT	30	CF6-50A	02-18-73		089,344		
064	47966	N602DA	DL	10	CF6-6D	11-10-72		082,906		
065	46524	N124AA	AA	10	CF6-6D	11-17-72		068,638		SPL
066	46753	N144US	NW	40	JT9D-20	12-12-72		069,475		
067	47967	N603DA	DL	10	CF6-6D	11-28-72		077,840		
068	46709	N67NA	NA	10	CF6-6D	11-30-72	STO	065,819		
069	47846	ZK-NZL	TE	30	CF6-50A	01-11-73	RET	061,332	10-21-88	
070	46710	N68N	NA	10	CF6-6D	12-12-72		076,817		
071	46552	PH-DTC	KL	30	CF6-50A	02-06-73		101,296		
072	46525	N125AA	AA	19	CF6-6D	12-19-72		072,189		
073	46576	HB-IHB	SR	30	CF6-50A	02-05-73		101,156		
074	47968	N604DA	DL	10	CF6-6D	01-05-73		082,414		
075	47861	I-DYNA	AZ	30	CF6-50A	02-06-73		076,417		
076	46615	N1816U	UA	10	CF6-6D	01-30-73		071,855		
077	46890	TU-TAL	RK	30	CF6-50A	02-28-73	W/O	083,878	12-21-99	
078	46907	TC-JAY	TK	10	CF6-6D	02-27-73		039,897		10F*
079	46754	N145US	NW	40	JT9D-20	01-31-73		069,227		

LN	MSN	REG	A/L	MODEL	ENG	DEL	STAT	HOURS	DATE	CVTD
080	47969	N605DA	DL	10	CF6-6D	02-16-73		080,407		
081	46825	N1031F	OV	30CF	CF6-50A	02-16-73	W/O	009,848	01-02-76	
082	46553	PH-DTD	KL	30	CF6-50A	02-28-73		094,136		
083	46727	G-BBSZ	GK	10	CF6-6D1	05-20-74		045,806		
084	46554	PH-DTE	KL	30	CF6-50A	03-09-73		083,182		
085	46851	F-BTDC	UT	30	CF6-50A	03-19-73		088,966		
086	46616	N1817U	UA	10	CF6-6D	03-22-73		070,839		
087	46925	EC-CBN	IB	30	CF6-50A	03-20-73	W/O	002,017	12-17-73	
088	47862	I-DYNE	AZ	30	CF6-50A	03-21-73		097,526		
089	46617	N1818U	UA	10	CF6-6D	04-06-73		058,753		
090	47886	9Q-CLI	QC	30	CF6-50A	06-08-73	STO	041,629	02-00-95	
091	46555	PH-DTF	KL	30	CF6-50A	04-13-73		098,954		
092	47800	N68046	CO	10	CF6-6D	04-12-73		082,753		
093	46852	N54629	UT	30	CF6-50A	05-01-73	W/O	060,291	09-19-89	
094	47863	I-DYNI	AZ	30	CF6-50A	04-20-73		099,750		
095	46908	N901WA	WA	10	CF6-6D	04-19-73		087,525		10F*
096	46800	N101TV	TV	30CF	CF6-50A	04-19-73		060,712		30F
097	46755	N146US	NW	40	JT9D-20	05-09-73		074,158		
098	47801	N68047	CO	10	CF6-6D	05-10-73		083,271		
099	46926	EC-CBO	IB	30	CF6-50A	05-19-73		092,731		
100	46927	EC-CBP	IB	30	CF6-50A	05-29-73		092,303		
101	47802	N68048	CO	10	CF6-6D	05-23-73	STO	062,091		10F*
102	46756	N147US	NW	40	JT9D-20	06-02-73		073,357		
103	46801	N102TV	TV	30CF	CF6-50A	06-04-73		062,960		30F
104	46928	N902WA	WA	10	CF6-6D	06-12-73	STO	061,140		
105	46711	N80NA	NA	30	CF6-50A	06-11-73	RET	074,831	05-12-93	
106	46712	N81NA	NA	30	CF6-50A	06-18-73		086,073		
107	46929	N903WA	WA	10	CF6-6D	06-21-73	W/O	024,617	10-31-79	
108	46757	N148US	NW	40	JT9D-20	07-06-73		075,666		
109	46826	N1032F	OV	30CF	CF6-50A	06-29-73	W/O	008,193	11-12-75	
110	46802	N103TV	TV	30CF	CF6-50A	07-02-73		059,059		30F
111	46758	N149US	NW	40	JT9D-20	07-25-73		076,149		
112	46930	N904WA	WA	10	CF6-6D	07-20-73		083,691		
113	46759	N150US	NW	40	JT9D-20	07-31-73		068,164		
114	46577	HB-IHC	SR	30	CF6-50A	09-10-73		107,849		
115	47906	OO-SLA	SN	30CF	CF6-50A	09-18-73		106,393		30F
116	47847	ZK-NZM	TE	30	CF6-50A	09-14-73		100,346		
117	47921	D-ADAO	LH	30	CF6-50A	11-12-73		090,933		30F
118	46618	N1819U	UA	10	CF6-6D	04-12-74	W/O	043,412	07-19-89	
119	46619	N1820U	UA	10	CF6-6D	02-22-74		059,627		10F*
120	46760	N151US	NW	40	JT9D-20	10-30-73		068,099		
121	47864	I-DYNO	AZ	30	CF6-50A	11-13-73		095,941		
122	47922	D-ADBO	LH	30	CF6-50A	01-15-74		087,239		30F
123	47923	D-ADCO	LH	30	CF6-50A	02-11-74		097,222		30F
124	46761	N152US	NW	40	JT9D-20	11-07-73		068,280		
125	47887	HS-VGE	YV	30	CF6-50C	11-25-74	W/O	011,362	07-27-89	
126	46762	N153US	NW	40	JT9D-20	11-14-73		069,171		
127	46891	PH-MBG	YM	30CF	CF6-50A	11-13-73		075,852		
128	46763	N154US	NW	40	JT9D-20	11-28-73		067,621		
129	47924	D-ADDO	LH	30	CF6-50A	02-15-74		096,317		30F
130	46764	N155US	NW	40	JT9D-20	12-12-73		068,830		
131	46578	HB-IHD	SR	30	CF6-50A	12-06-73		088,655		
132	46579	HB-IHE	SR	30	CF6-50A	02-06-74		104,390		
133	46944	PP-VMA	VG	30	CF6-50C	05-29-74		081,904		
134	46853	N54639	UT	30	CF6-50A	01-18-74		091,520		
135	47865	I-DYNU	AZ	30	CF6-50A	01-22-74		091,820		
136	47848	ZK-NZN	TE	30	CF6-50A	01-18-74		098,872		
137	46931	AP-AXC	PK	30	CF6-50C	03-01-74		067,365		
138	46620	N1821U	UA	10	CF6-6D	02-13-74		059,483		MD10
139	47803	N68049	CO	10CF	CF6-6D	02-04-74		050,380		10F*
140	46621	N1822U	UA	10	CF6-6D	04-25-74		059,600		10F*
141	46940	AP-AXD	PK	30	CF6-50C	04-02-74		082,078		
142	47804	N68050	CO	10CF	CF6-6D	03-04-74		049,147		10F*
143	46765	N156US	NW	40	JT9D-20	03-08-74		073,712		

LN	MSN	REG	A/L	MODEL	ENG	DEL	STAT	HOURS	DATE	CVTD
144	46622	N1823U	UA	10	CF6-6D	05-02-74		063,795		10F*
145	47805	N68051	CO	10CF	CF6-6D	04-08-74		056,335		10F*
146	46556	PH-DTG	KL	30	CF6-50A	04-03-74		085,758		
147	46936	XA-DUG	AM	30	CF6-50C	04-17-74		075,196		
148	47806	N68052	CO	10CF	CF6-6D	04-11-74		052,312		10F*
149	47866	I-DYNB	AZ	30	CF6-50A	04-19-74		090,148		
150	47980	EC-CEZ	IB	30	CF6-50A	05-19-74		093,303		
151	46766	N157US	NW	40	JT9D-20	05-17-74		066,858		
152	46937	XA-DUH	AM	30	CF6-50C	05-16-74		074,907		
153	46938	N905WA	WA	10	CF6-6D	05-14-74		079,710		
154	46623	N1824U	UA	10	CF6-6D	06-19-74		061,467		
155	46624	N1825U	UA	10	CF6-6D	06-26-74		064,453		10F*
156	46945	PP-VMB	VG	30	CF6-50C	06-18-74		082,718		
157	47907	OO-SLB	SN	30CF	CF6-50A	06-10-74		089,056		SPL
158	46932	9Q-CLT	QC	30	CF6-50A	06-26-74		068,031		30F
159	46933	PH-DTI	PR	30	CF6-50C	06-27-74		085,703		
160	46934	HL7315	KE	30	CF6-50C	06-20-74		067,056		
161	46767	N158US	NW	40	JT9D-20	07-19-74		071,311		
162	46942	N69NA	NA	10	CF6-6D	06-25-75		061,472		
163	46943	N70NA	NA	10	CF6-6D	06-23-75		071,850		
164	46768	N159US	NW	40	JT9D-20	08-09-74		065,936		
165	46713	N82NA	NA	30	CF6-50A	06-20-75		082,399		
166	47925	D-ADFO	LH	30	CF6-50A	11-14-74		095,191		30F
167	46714	N83NA	NA	30	CF6-50A	06-16-75		077,660		
168	46769	N160US	NW	40	JT9D-20	09-10-74		072,026		
169	46625	N1826U	UA	10	CF6-6D	02-27-75		062,204		10F*
170	47926	D-ADGO	LH	30	CF6-50A	01-03-75		098,147		
171	46868	LN-RKA	SK	30	CF6-50A	10-01-74		103,169		
172	46935	AP-AXE	PK	30	CF6-50C	10-19-74	W/O	017,970	02-02-81	
173	47807	N68053	CO	10CF	CF6-6D	02-18-75		052,270		10F*
174	46869	SE-DFD	SK	30	CF6-50A	11-04-74		102,557		
175	46770	N161US	NW	40	JT9D-20	11-05-74		072,676		
176	46941	PP-VMQ	VG	30	CF6-50C	11-07-74		083,118		
177	47808	N68054	CO	10CF	CF6-6D	03-10-75		044,146		10F*
178	47867	I-DYNC	AZ	30	CF6-50A	02-18-75		080,215		
179	46949	G-BEBL	BR	30	CF6-50C	03-31-77		088,034		
180	46771	N162US	NW	40	JT9D-20	12-06-74		066,190		
181	47956	OH-LHA	AY	30	CF6-50C	01-27-75		089,137		
182	46910	ZK-NZP	TE	30	CF6-50C	12-13-74	W/O	020,757	11-28-79	
183	46580	HB-IHF	SR	30	CF6-50A	01-11-75		103,781		
184	46581	HB-IHG	SR	30	CF6-50A	02-14-75		102,332		
185	46952	PH-DTL	PR	30	CF6-50A	02-26-75		088,328		
186	47981	EC-CLB	IB	30	CF6-50A	01-24-75		090,099		
187	46582	HB-IHH	SR	30	CF6-50A	02-21-75		101,481		
188	46912	HL7316	KE	30	CF6-50C	02-07-75		071,208		
189	46911	ZK-NZQ	TE	30	CF6-50C	02-20-75		089,683		
190	47927	D-ADHO	LH	30	CF6-50A	02-28-75		103,730		
191	47809	N68055	CO	10CF	CF6-6D	03-17-75		038,266		10F*
192	47928	D-ADJO	LH	30	CF6-50A	03-10-75		099,950		
193	46854	N54649	UT	30	CF6-50A	03-19-75		090,683		
194	47810	N68056	CO	10CF	CF6-6D	03-24-75		053,362		10F*
195	46914	PH-DTK	PR	30	CF6-50C	03-27-75		095,055		
196	47929	D-ADKO	LH	30	CF6-50A	03-31-75		094,721		30F
197	46557	PH-DTH	VA	30	CF6-50A	04-15-75	RET	082,642	07-30-98	
198	46626	N1827U	UA	10	CF6-6D	04-25-75		062,779		10F*
199	46915	HL7317	KE	30	CF6-50C	04-25-75		071,409		
200	47868	I-DYND	AZ	30	CF6-50A	05-05-75		076,489		
201	47957	OH-LHB	AY	30	CF6-50C	05-06-75		093,380		
202	46916	PP-VMD	RG	30	CF6-50C	06-12-75		078,998		
203	46939	N906WA	WA	10	CF6-6D	06-03-75		077,358		
204	46892	TU-TAM	RK	30	CF6-50A	06-19-75		083,620		
205	46627	N1828U	UA	10	CF6-6D	06-23-75		072,798		
206	46913	JA8534	JL	40-I	JT9D-59A	11-23-76		060,108		
207	46628	N1829U	UA	10	CF6-6D	07-24-75		071,684		

LN	MSN	REG	A/L	MODEL	ENG	DEL	STAT	HOURS	DATE	CVTD
208	46629	N1830U	UA	10	CF6-6D	08-04-75		063,886		
209	46630	N1831U	UA	10	CF6-6D	08-20-75		063,956		10F*
210	46631	N1832U	UA	10	CF6-6D	09-23-75		061,533		10F*
211	46917	D-ADLO	LH	30	CF6-50C	12-01-75		093,317		
212	46920	JA8530	JL	40-D	JT9D-59A	04-09-76		050,270		40F
213	47849	ZK-NZR	TE	30	CF6-50C	10-02-75		079,908		
214	46921	G-BEBM	BR	30	CF6-50C	02-23-77		086,874		
215	47908	OO-SLC	SN	30CF	CF6-50C	10-27-75		085,054		30F
216	46923	JA8531	JL	40-D	JT9D-59A	04-12-76		048,062		
217	46870	OY-KDA	SK	30	CF6-50A	12-18-75		093,472		
218	46924	PH-MBN	YM	30CF	CF6-50C	11-26-75	W/O	061,414	12-21-92	
219	46871	LN-RKB	SK	30	CF6-50C	01-23-76		068,358		30F
220	46660	JA8532	JL	40-D	JT9D-59A	04-16-76		050,880		
221	46922	EC-CSJ	IB	30	CF6-50C	02-23-76		085,995		
222	46946	N907WA	WA	10	CF6-6D	06-22-76		055,234		
223	46918	PK-GIA	GA	30	CF6-50C	03-22-76		068,331		
224	46661	JA8533	JL	40-D	JT9D-59A	05-25-76		049,605		40F
225	46953	EC-CSK	IB	30	CF6-50C	05-14-76		087,704		
226	46919	PK-GIB	GA	30	CF6-50C	05-29-76		067,827		
227	46954	ZK-NZS	TE	30	CF6-50C	06-07-76		081,055		
228	46955	9M-MAS	MH	30	CF6-50C	08-02-76		066,946		30F
229	47889	AP-AYM	PK	30	CF6-50C	08-25-76		070,689		
230	46662	JA8535	JL	40-I	JT9D-59A	08-13-76		067,775		
231	46957	5N-ANN	WT	30	CF6-50C	10-14-76		058,937		
232	46958	RCP2003	PR	30	CF6-50C	10-22-76		071,583		
233	46872	SE-DFE	SK	30	CF6-50C	12-02-76		090,842		
234	46959	HS-TGD	TG	30	CF6-50C	03-03-77		075,412		
235	46956	PH-MBP	YM	30CF	CF6-50C	12-23-76		068,520		KDC10
236	46961	HS-TGE	TG	30	CF6-50C	05-05-77		079,483		
237	46960	N1033F	OV	30CF	CF6-50C1	05-09-77	W/O	024,760	12-23-83	
238	46962	N1034F	OV	30CF	CF6-50C1	06-06-77	W/O	015,366	09-13-82	
239	46964	PK-GIC	GA	30	CF6-50C	10-03-77		060,482		
240	46640	9M-MAT	MH	30	CF6-50C	09-21-77		071,665		
241	46969	HB-IHI	SR	30	CF6-50C	10-21-77		090,880		
242	46950	ZK-NZI	TE	30	CF6-50C	11-10-77		070,575		
243	46968	5N-ANR	WT	30	CF6-50C	10-18-77	W/O	029,487	01-10-87	
244	46963	F-BTDD	UT	30	CF6-50C	11-02-77		080,602		
245	46965	D-ADMO	LH	30	CF6-50C	12-09-77		081,251		30F
246	46951	PK-GID	GA	30	CF6-50C	01-13-78		059,437		
247	46947	N126AA	AA	10	CF6-6D	02-10-78		069,190		
248	46975	N103WA	WO	30CF	CF6-50C1	03-07-78		078,339		
249	46948	N127AA	AA	10	CF6-6D	03-20-78		066,017		
250	46984	N128AA	AA	10	CF6-6D	05-01-78		068,282		
251	46977	N908WA	WA	10	CF6-6D	03-13-78		062,658		
252	46983	N909WA	WA	10	CF6-6D	05-18-78		069,922		
253	46986	N104WA	WO	30CF	CF6-50C1	06-15-78		076,599		
254	46976	C-GXRB	WD	30	CF6-50C1	12-14-78		057,441		
255	46987	N105WA	WO	30	CF6-50C1	08-04-78		076,109		
256	46978	C-GXRC	WD	30	CF6-50C1	11-03-78		060,131		30F
257	46992	N1035F	OV	30CF	CF6-50C1	09-08-78		050,840		30F
258	46971	YV135C	VA	30	CF6-50C	09-21-78	RET	055,402	03-22-94	
259	46981	YU-ANA	JU	30	CF6-50C1	12-08-78		072,436		
260	46990	9V-SDA	SQ	30	CF6-50C1	10-23-78		066,389		
261	46991	9V-SDC	SQ	30	CF6-50C1	01-31-79		078,081		
262	46966	JA8536	JL	40-D	JT9D-59A	11-20-78		044,557		
263	46993	9V-SDB	SQ	30	CF6-50C1	11-29-78		067,515		
264	46985	PH-MBT	YM	30CF	CF6-50C	12-20-78		062,422		KDC10
265	46967	JA8537	JL	40-D	JT9D-59A	01-18-79		045,705		
266	46590	G-BFGI	BR	30	CF6-50C	01-22-79		089,619		
267	46998	HB-IHK	YB	30	CF6-50	01-31-79		065,213		
268	46540	C-GCPC	CP	30	CF6-50C1	03-27-79		086,407		
269	46970	G-GFAL	GK	10	CF6-6D1	02-27-79		039,041		10F*
270	46996	N129AA	AA	10	CF6-6D	02-27-79		063,774		
271	46989	N130AA	AA	10	CF6-6D	03-15-79		063,539		10*

LN	MSN	REG	A/L	MODEL	ENG	DEL	STAT	HOURS	DATE	CVTD
272	46973	G-GSKY	GK	10	CF6-6D1	03-21-79		039,476		10F*
273	46994	N131AA	AA	10	CF6-6D	04-03-79		063,958		
274	46974	JA8538	JL	40-I	JT9D-59A	04-04-79		065,470		
275	46995	9V-SDD	SQ	30	CF6-50C1	03-30-79		067,784		
276	46972	YV136C	VA	30	CF6-50C	04-20-79		066,905		
277	46835	N106WA	WO	30CF	CF6-50C2	04-27-79		062,965		30F
278	46988	YU-AMB	JU	30	CF6-50C1	05-14-79		055,691		
279	47982	EX-DEA	IB	30	CF6-50C	05-14-79		076,881		
280	46836	N107WA	WO	30CF	CF6-50C2	05-21-79		065,999		
281	46541	C-GCPD	CP	30	CF6-50C1	07-19-79		083,567		
282	46837	N108WA	WO	30CF	CF6-50C2	05-29-79		060,776		30F
283	46645	N912WA	WA	10	CF6-6D	07-19-79		056,710		
284	46685	PK-GIE	GA	30	CF6-50C	07-27-79	W/O	046,318	06-13-96	
285	46646	N913WA	WA	10	CF6-6D	07-26-79		065,257		
286	46686	PK-GIF	GA	30	CF6-50C	08-22-79		054,361		
287	46591	G-BGAT	BR	30	CF6-50C	08-08-79		088,767		
288	46997	TU-TAN	RK	30	CF6-50C	08-10-79		068,049		
289	46999	9V-SDE	SQ	30	CF6-50C2	08-29-79		059,819		
290	46982	YV137C	VA	30	CF6-50C	10-05-79		069,693		
291	47888	YA-LAS	FG	30	CF6-50C2	09-21-79		064,419		
292	46583	HB-IHL	SR	30	CF6-50C	03-03-80		081,773		
293	46584	HB-IHM	SR	30	CF6-50C	02-01-80		084,289		
294	47827	N132AA	AA	10	CF6-6D	11-13-79		063,371		10*
295	46542	C-GCPE	CP	30	CF6-50C2	11-02-79		081,913		
296	46632	N1838U	UA	10	CF6-6D	11-30-79	STO	063,315		
297	46633	N1839U	UA	10	CF6-6D	02-15-80		064,799		
298	46634	N1841U	UA	10	CF6-6D	01-31-80		061,315		
299	46595	D-ADPO	YD	30	CF6-50C2	11-21-79		067,147		
300	47817	PP-VMR	SQ	30	CF6-50C2	11-30-79		065,582		
301	46959	D-ADQO	YD	30	CF6-50C2	12-15-79		067,223		
302	47811	G-BGXE	GK	30	CF6-50C2	12-15-79		065,552		
303	47812	G-BGXF	GK	30	CF6-50C2	01-05-80		064,773		
304	47822	JA8539	JA	40-I	JT9D-59A	01-07-80		065,514		
305	47818	PP-VMS	SQ	30	CF6-50C2	01-25-80		061,552		
306	47823	JA8540	JL	40-D	JT9D-59A	12-24-79		042,934		
307	46635	N1842U	UA	10	CF6-6D	02-28-80		062,958		
308	47824	JA8541	JL	40-I	JT9D-59A	03-20-80		059,916		
309	46636	N1843U	UA	10	CF6-6D	03-14-80		062,883		
310	47825	JA8542	JL	40-I	JT9D-59A	04-17-80		055,062		
311	48200	79-0433	ZA	KC-10	CF6-50C2	10-01-81		014,903		
312	47813	G-BGXG	GK	30	CF6-50C2	03-24-80		064,470		
313	47826	JA8543	JL	40-I	JT9D-59A	05-22-80		059,853		
314	47819	N109WA	WO	30CF	CF6-50C2	04-09-80		073,804		30F
315	47814	G-BGXH	GK	30	CF6-50C2	04-30-80		066,346		
316	47816	G-BHDH	BR	30	CF6-50C	04-30-80		082,941		
317	47820	N112WA	WO	30CF	CF6-50C2	05-14-80		062,206		30F
318	47832	N914WA	WA	10	CF6-6D	05-12-80		063,759		
319	47828	N133A	AA	10	CF6-6D	05-15-80		059,060		
320	47821	N113WA	WO	30	CF6-50C2	05-27-80	W/O	006,325	01-23-82	
321	47829	N134AA	AA	10	CF6-6D	05-23-80		063,051		10*
322	47833	N915WA	WA	10	CF6-6D	06-05-80		062,698		
323	47830	N135AA	AA	10	CF6-6D	06-09-80		061,753		
324	47834	EC-DHZ	IB	30	CF6-50C	06-23-80		074,873		
325	47815	G-BGXI	GK	30	CF6-50C2	06-24-80		066,142		
326	47835	OO-SLD	SN	30CF	CF6-50C2	07-09-80		067,788		30F
327	47831	G-BHDI	BR	30	CF6-50C	07-21-80		079,689		
328	47837	N84NA	NA	30	CF6-50C	08-06-80		061,572		
329	47841	PP-VMT	RG	30	CF6-50C2	07-31-80		061,714		30F
330	47836	OO-SLE	SN	30CF	CF6-50C2	08-14-80		066,528		30F
331	47850	N68060	CO	30	CF6-50C2	08-28-80		087,456		
332	47842	PP-VMU	RG	30	CF6-50C2	09-05-80		061,596		30F
333	48201	79-0434	ZA	KC-10	CF6-50C2	03-17-81		014,697		
334	47851	N12061	CO	30	CF6-50C2	09-25-80		085,774		
335	47843	PP-VMV	RG	30	CF6-50C2	10-09-80		067,283		

LN	MSN	REG	A/L	MODEL	ENG	DEL	STAT	HOURS	DATE	CVTD
336	47844	PP-VMW	RG	30	CF6-50C2	11-10-80		062,817		
337	47840	G-BHDJ	BR	30	CF6-50C	10-16-80		077,458		
338	47838	RPC2114	PR	30	CF6-50C2	11-25-80		059,971		
339	47870	N305FE	FM	30CF	CF6-50C2	09-07-84		035,741		30F
340	47852	JA8544	JL	40-I	JT9D-59A	12-09-80		063,758		
341	46543	C-GCPF	CP	30	CF6-50C2	11-26-80		075,696		
342	48252	D-ADSO	YD	30	CF6-50C2	01-22-81		062,191		
343	47853	JA8545	JL	40-I	JT9D-59A	12-19-80		051,626		
344	48260	N1844U	UA	10	CF6-6D	04-09-81		060,745		
345	48265	N345HC	AY	30	CF6-50C2	08-11-81		062,895		
346	48258	N1003L	MX	15	CF6-50C2	06-15-81		037,898		
347	48261	N1845U	UA	10	CF6-6D	04-24-81		056,988		
348	48266	N3016Z	QZ	30	CF6-50C2	07-20-84		048,083		
349	47855	JA8546	JL	40-D	JT9D-59A	03-25-81		040,957		
350	48283	9M-MAV	MH	30	CF6-50C2	02-20-81		053,057		
351	48262	N1846U	UA	10	CF6-6D	05-08-81		061,324		
352	48285	C-GCPG	CP	30	CF6-50C2	02-27-81		076,722		
353	48263	N1847U	UA	10	CF6-6D	05-22-81		056,819		
354	48277	G-DCIO	BR	30	CF6-50C2	04-15-81		075,660		
355	48282	PP-VMY	RG	30	CF6-50C2	04-30-81		065,525		
356	47845	PP-VMX	RG	30	CF6-50C2	06-03-81		066,444		
357	48259	N10045	MX	15	CF6-50C2	06-29-81		040,630		
358	48275	N10038	AM	15	CF6-50C2	06-30-81		039,413		
359	48202	79-1710	ZA	KC10	CF6-50C2	07-30-81		014,594		
360	48203	79-1711	ZA	KC10	CF6-50C2	08-28-81		014,714		
361	48204	79-1712	ZA	KC10	CF6-50C2	09-22-81		015,499		
362	48276	N1003N	AM	15	CF6-50C2	11-21-81		041,049		
363	48205	79-1713	ZA	KC10	CF6-50C2	10-23-81		015,081		
364	48288	C-GCPH	CP	30	CF6-50C2	11-02-81		074,386		
365	48289	N1003W	MX	15	CF6-50C2	12-03-81		042,293		
366	47856	JA8547	JL	40-I	JT9D-59A	12-08-81		058,368		
367	47857	JA8548	JL	40-D	JT9D-59A	01-25-82		038,710		
368	48292	HB-IHN	SR	30	CF6-50C2	02-27-82		079,458		
369	48286	9G-ANA	GH	30	CF6-50C2	02-25-83		052,442		
370	48296	C-GCPI	CP	30	CF6-50C2	02-19-82		072,116		
371	48293	HB-IHO	SR	30	CF6-50C2	04-01-82		078,039		
372	48294	XA-MEW	MX	15	CF6-50C2	01-13-83		034,250		
373	48206	79-1946	ZA	KC10	CF6-50C2	05-25-82		014,572		
374	48295	XA-MEX	MX	15	CF6-50C2	01-13-83		038,796		
375	48207	79-1947	ZA	KC10	CF6-50C2	06-21-82		013,816		
376	48208	79-1948	ZA	KC10	CF6-50C2	07-23-82		014,139		
377	48209	79-1949	ZA	KC10	CF6-50C2	08-09-82		014,341		
378	48210	79-1950	ZA	KC10	CF6-50C2	09-08-82		014,266		
379	48264	N1848U	UA	10CF	CF6-6D	09-20-82		041,974		10F*
380	48211	79-1951	ZA	KC10	CF6-50C2	11-18-82		013,165		
381	48301	JA8549	JL	40-D	JT9D-59A	03-15-83		036,388		
382	48212	82-0190	ZA	KC10	CF6-50C2	04-06-83	W/O	003,523	09-17-87	
383	48213	82-0191	ZA	KC10	CF6-50C2	04-19-83		012,994		
384	48214	82-0192	ZA	KC10	CF6-50C2	05-20-83		013,656		
385	48215	82-0193	ZA	KC10	CF6-50C2	07-28-83		013,248		
386	48216	83-0075	ZA	KC10	CF6-50C2	08-23-83		011,810		
387	48217	83-0076	ZA	KC10	CF6-50C2	09-16-83		014,176		
388	48218	83-0077	ZA	KC10	CF6-50C2	11-02-83		012,589		
389	48219	83-0078	ZA	KC10	CF6-50C2	12-13-83		013,287		
390	48220	83-0079	ZA	KC10	CF6-50C2	02-27-84		012,185		
391	48221	83-0080	ZA	KC10	CF6-50C2	03-28-84		013,893		
392	48222	83-0081	ZA	KC10	CF6-50C2	06-07-84		012,709		
393	48223	83-0082	ZA	KC10	CF6-50C2	07-19-84		013,295		
394	48224	84-0185	ZA	KC10	CF6-50C2	09-04-84		013,021		
395	48225	84-0186	ZA	KC10	CF6-50C2	10-15-84		012,430		
396	48226	84-0187	ZA	KC10	CF6-50C2	11-27-84		012,982		
397	48227	84-0188	ZA	KC10	CF6-50C2	12-19-84		012,193		
398	48228	84-0189	ZA	KC10	CF6-50C2	02-05-85		011,238		
399	48229	84-0190	ZA	KC10	CF6-50C2	03-16-85		012,394		

LN	MSN	REG	A/L	MODEL	ENG	DEL	STAT	HOURS	DATE	CVTD
400	48230	84-0191	ZA	KC10	CF6-50C2	04-18-85		012,831		
401	48231	84-0192	ZA	KC10	CF6-50C2	06-04-85		011,904		
402	48232	85-0027	ZA	KC10	CF6-50C2	08-21-85		011,872		
403	48233	85-0028	ZA	KC10	CF6-50C2	08-01-85		011,179		
404	48234	84-0029	ZA	KC10	CF6-50C2	09-04-85		012,479		
405	48235	84-0030	ZA	KC10	CF6-50C2	09-19-85		012,608		
406	48236	85-0031	ZA	KC10	CF6-50C2	10-10-85		012,177		
407	48237	85-0032	ZA	KC10	CF6-50C2	11-04-85		012,382		
408	48238	85-0033	ZA	KC10	CF6-50C2	12-03-85		012,465		
409	48287	N306FE	FM	30F	CF6-50C2	01-24-86		034,298		
410	48239	85-0034	ZA	KC10	CF6-50C2	02-04-86		011,642		
411	48240	86-0027	ZA	KC10	CF6-50C2	02-27-86		011,334		
412	48291	N307FE	FM	30F	CF6-50C2	03-07-86		035,077		
413	48241	86-0028	ZA	KC10	CF6-50C2	03-29-86		012,530		
414	48242	86-0029	ZA	KC10	CF6-50C2	04-25-86		012,449		
415	48243	86-0030	ZA	KC10	CF6-50C2	05-09-86		012,729		
416	48297	N308FE	FM	30F	CF6-50C2	05-28-86		034,265		
417	48244	86-0031	ZA	KC10	CF6-50C2	06-23-86		011,548		
418	48245	86-0032	ZA	KC10	CF6-50C2	07-18-86		012,126		
419	49298	N309FE	FM	30F	CF6-50C2	07-31-86		033,639		
420	48246	86-0033	ZA	KC10	CF6-50C2	08-27-86		011,792		
421	48247	86-0034	ZA	KC10	CF6-50C2	09-30-86		012,153		
422	48299	N310FE	FM	30F	CF6-50C2	09-30-86		033,317		
423	48248	86-0035	ZA	KC10	CF6-50C2	10-31-86		011,353		
424	48249	86-0036	ZA	KC10	CF6-50C2	11-30-86		011,838		
425	48250	86-0037	ZA	KC10	CF6-50C2	12-24-86		010,893		
426	48251	86-0038	ZA	KC10	CF6-50C2	01-31-87		011,829		
427	48303	87-0117	ZA	KC10	CF6-50C2	02-28-87		010,754		
428	48304	87-0118	ZA	KC10	CF6-50C2	04-17-87		011,010		
429	48305	87-0119	ZA	KC10	CF6-50C2	05-26-87		011,161		
430	48306	87-0120	ZA	KC10	CF6-50C2	06-30-87		009,675		
431	48307	87-0121	ZA	KC10	CF6-50C2	08-21-87		011,790		
432	48308	87-0122	ZA	KC10	CF6-50C2	11-17-87		010,776		
433	48300	N312FE	FM	30F	CF6-50C2	09-30-87		031,991		
434	48267	HS-TMA	TG	30	CF6-50C2	12-01-87		036,755		
435	48290	HS-TMB	TG	30	CF6-50C2	12-22-87		036,573		
436	48315	JA8550	JD	30	CF6-50C2	03-30-88		022,756		
437	48316	JA8551	JD	30	CF6-50C2	07-29-88		022,977		
438	48319	HS-TMC	TG	30	CF6-50C2	05-26-88		032,772		
439	48309	87-0123	ZA	KC10	CF6-50C2	08-24-88		009,754		
440	48311	N313FE	FM	30F	CF6-50C2	05-28-88		029,478		
441	48310	87-0124	ZA	KC10	CF6-50C2	09-30-88		008,335		
442	48312	N314FE	FM	30F	CF6-50C2	08-26-88		028,128		
443	48313	N315FE	FM	30F	CF6-50C2	09-29-88		028,850		
444	48314	N316FE	FM	30F	CF6-50C2	10-28-88		027,527		
445	48317	S2-ACR	BG	30	CF6-50C2	12-30-88		038,919		
446	48318	5N-AUI	WT	30	CF6-50C2	07-27-89		025,774		

Series 30F N315FE (ln 443/msn 48313) in the 1994 FedEx livery. (Tim Ihle)